STO
ACPL
P9-BHR-587
DISCARDED

8-23-65

195x

Race Relations and Christian Mission

Race Relations and Christian Mission

by DAISUKE KITAGAWA

FRIENDSHIP PRESS
NEW YORK

CIRCULATION DEPARTMENT
PUBLIC LIBRARY
FORT WAYNE & ALLEN CO., IND.

All Bible quotations used in this book are from the Revised Standard Version, copyright, 1946 and 1952, by the Division of Christian Education of the National Council of the Churches of Christ in the United States of America.

Library of Congress Catalog Card Number: 64-11007

Copyright © 1964 by Friendship Press, Inc.
Printed in the United States of America

Contents

1340937

Race Relations and Christian Mission

PREFACE

Why another book on race relations? In the area of race relations what the church needs is more action and less talk! To this I agree whole-heartedly. Still I have consented to write this small volume because I felt that, despite all the anguish and striving of the last decade or so, we Christians in this great republic still have a great deal more to learn in order to know *how to think* about and cope with the racial and ethnic tensions which remain prevalent in our own society and in the world today.

This book is more about the church caught in the current racial crisis than about race. What is paramount in the author's concern is how the church can be the church in the contemporary world in which racial and ethnic tensions happen to be one of the most crucial factors. Seen from this vantage point, the phenomena of racial and ethnic tensions present, in the first instance, a sociological context in which the church has to witness to the gospel. There is, however, also an ethical issue to which the church must address herself with a clear and unequivocal voice. If the church fails in coming to terms with the problem of racial and ethnic tensions in those two different, though mutually related, dimensions, it can hardly claim to be the church in the contemporary world. In saying this I am assuming that the theme of Oxford, 1937 (World Conference on Life and Work), "Let the Church be the Church," implies that the church must be the church within the context of the world and not outside.

The term "race" disturbs not a few people who seek scientific accuracy. There is a sense in which there is no such thing as a race save the human race, but from our vocabulary we do not seem to be able to eliminate the term completely. Throughout the book "race" is used in a commonly accepted sense, referring to the three major anthropological classifications, Caucasoid, Mongoloid, and Negroid, and the term "ethnic" is used to indicate most of the lesser groupings within a racial group such as national and tribal. In strictly vernacular usage it may be said that the two terms are used almost interchangeably.

The book may be divided into three sections. The first three chapters describe the problem of racial and ethnic tensions as an ethical issue within the author's own experience. The following three chapters describe the historical background and the sociological context, in the light of which the race problem needs to be seen, if it is to be thoroughly understood for what it really is. Chapters 7-9 constitute an analytical section in which the author attempts to assess critically why we have racial and ethnic tensions today; why the church has so far failed in coming to grips with them; and what is demanded of the church in order to be the church in reference to this particular problem. The Epilogue is added to present the church's teaching on human and intergroup relations in biblical terms.

The author expresses his gratitude to the Commission on

PREFACE

Missionary Education, National Council of the Churches of Christ in the U.S.A., for the invitation to write this volume; to Dr. J. Oscar Lee, Director, Department of Racial and Cultural Relations, National Council of the Churches of Christ in the U.S.A., for his guidance and encouragement over the past two decades in coping with the complex problem of race relations; to the World Council of Churches for having provided me with opportunities to learn at first hand in many parts of the world about many different patterns of the racial and ethnic problems and a wide range of issues involved therein.

The author is indebted to his colleague and friend the Rev. Robert MacGill, for going over the first draft and making innumerable suggestions, without which many a part of the book would have remained well-nigh unintelligible to its readers. I would be less than human if I failed to acknowledge publicly how much my wife and children have contributed to the production of this volume by cheerfully keeping the home-fires burning during my frequent and many-weeks-long journeys abroad. Finally a word of profound appreciation is due to my secretary Miss Sharon Walworth for preparing a typescript from my hand-written manuscript under a terrific pressure of time.

DAISUKE KITAGAWA

CHAPTER 1

Ethnic Minorities Come of Age

Voice of African Christian Leaders, 1960

In October, 1960, I found myself as a house guest of Mr. and Mrs. Grant in Salisbury, Southern Rhodesia. Jack Grant, born and reared in the West Indies, and his wife Ida, an Afrikaner from South Africa, are a missionary couple and, in 1960, were on the staff of the American Board of Commissioners for Foreign Missions. Jack is a professional educator, ex-Principal of Adams College (South Africa), a layman of British Congregationalist upbringing. I am an Episcopal priest, a naturalized U.S. citizen of Japanese background, and, at the time of the visit, secretary in the Study Division of the World Council of Churches based in Geneva, Switzerland.

Only the night before I had left Geneva and was met by Jack at the Salisbury Airport early in the morning. We had not previously known each other but within a few hours I felt as though I had known him and his wife for years. This was one of many occasions in my life that brought home to me what the church is or what being a part of the church means. The three persons sitting at the breakfast table on that morning represented the most complex variety of things that so often separate men from one another. But here we were truly one. This is a reality of the church today (as it has always been), and this reality is being experienced everywhere in the world—yes, in spite of many things which appear to refute it, some of which will be told in this volume. But here I want it remembered by my readers that everything I am going to say in the following pages is said within the context of this empirically felt reality of Christian fellowship.

While at Salisbury I wanted to hear the voice of African people.[1] On the day set aside for my visit to the Harare Location outside of Salisbury, however, Jack unfortunately had to be out of town to visit one of the missions under his charge. Accompanied by Ida, I went there to be received by a group of African pastors of several denominations. Before the meeting was opened Ida said to the group, "You probably would like to talk with Mr. Kitagawa without me, and I want you to do so, too." In answer they all said, "We won't mind your presence at all. We shall be just as frank with our visitor with you around. There is nothing which we will be embarrassed to say in your presence. Please stay." The ensuing two hours more than proved that they meant what they said. Here was another concrete example of the Christian fellowship that transcends everything which in many other contexts constitute barriers to keep men separate one from another.

The meeting soon got under way following a short period of worship. Everybody was polite and proper. Nothing spectacular was said or done by anybody. The meeting was

[1] In Africa, African means Negro, Colored means Euro-African, and European means white.

frankly dull but I knew that I was being sized up by everybody present. (Incidentally I learned how important this period of beating around the bush is in the process of knowing one another, especially between people of different backgrounds. I had had some bitter experiences of being entirely misunderstood by being completely open and straightforward.) I have a sneaking suspicion that my imperfect English—neither Queen's nor American but foreigner's English—was more instrumental than any other asset I might have had to establish a sense of kinship between us. Presently I seem to have been sized up as a visiting churchman who is better at listening to them than talking to them, and my questions were heard exactly as they were meant. Honest and frank conversation became possible as no one was inclined to look under the rug everytime anybody said anything.

In the course of the conversation I asked: From what I have so far learned, most of the leaders in the African nationalist movement now on the blacklist of the Colonial Government were either educated in mission schools or used to be members of churches of one denomination or another. Is this correct? And, if so, what do you regard as your responsibility towards them? Do you feel that you still have pastoral responsibilities over them, or do you regard them as apostates and forget them? As churchmen do you dissociate yourselves from the African nationalist movement led by them? By the time I finished stating my question practically everybody in the circle was on his feet to speak. Any sign of dullness completely disappeared and an extremely lively session lasted well over an hour, the gist of which may be summarized as follows:

Those nationalist leaders who are labeled as "troublemakers," "extremists," and the like were almost without exception educated—or at least received their earliest education—in the mission schools. Otherwise they could not have been what they now are, for until quite recently there were only mission schools to give any sort of education to Africans. Many of those now active in politics are known to have been at one time or another members of the Christian churches but most of them have not been active in the churches in recent years. They all seem to feel that they had been rejected or at least let down by the churches. The church has alienated them rather than the reverse. We pastors are one with them for we know that they are risking their lives to put into practice what we have been preaching all these years without the courage to act according to our words. As far as we are concerned, they are still within the church and we not only have pastoral responsibility over them but we are prepared to follow them even into jail.

The pastors went on, unprompted by questions from me, to say that they could no longer count on the missionaries from overseas or their white colleagues as far as the future of the African people was concerned. For, they said, in a showdown "the white brethren will be law-abiding citizens of the Colony rather than the prophetic ministers of the gospel." They then added: "We do not expect them to stick their necks out for the sake of the gospel at the expense of their personal safety, not to mention their lives. That would be too much to expect of them. We only mean that in the final analysis we have to take our own destiny in our own hands, both as Christians and as Africans. We cannot and will not depend on what other people would do for us." They said this, I must hasten to add, without any sign of bitterness, anger, or self-righteousness. It was a totally unsolicited remark made in the most matter-of-fact manner, betraying only a deep sense of disappointment in those with whom they had toiled for so many years.

When I later reported on this prevailing sentiment among African churchmen I was severely criticized by the representatives of the missionary forces. That African Christians, and more especially pastors, would say such a thing was to them totally inconceivable. "How dare they say such a thing about us! You must be exaggerating their feelings on the basis of critical remarks made by some extremists." Such was the attitude expressed by many of the missionaries, both British and American. One can see how little genuine communication had been taking place between European and African Christians in that part of the world, and the frightful thing about it is that this breakdown of communication was not of recent origin or due to ill-will on either side but had existed for many a decade in spite of genuine good-will on the part of both European and African Christian leadership toward each other. Somehow the two racial communities had been living in two different, and mutually unrelated, worlds, even within the context of the Christian church.

Voice of Negro Leaders in the U.S. South, 1959

This encounter with an honest expression of the unvarnished sentiment of the African Christians and political leaders toward the Europeans among them vividly reminded me of the conversations I had had during the previous year in the southern states of the U.S.A. with a number of Negro Christian leaders.

It was in October and November of 1959 that I visited such urban centers as Nashville and Memphis, Tennessee; Little Rock, Arkansas; Montgomery, Alabama; Atlanta, Georgia; etc. They were chosen to be on my itinerary either as places where critical incidents had taken place within the recent past or as seats of leadership. From the vantage point of 1963 it is important to point out that those were days prior even to the college students' sit-in demonstrations.

A new era was dawning on the South nevertheless. The success of the mass boycott of the Montgomery City Bus System by the Negro citizens under the leadership of Dr. Martin Luther King and his colleagues (not all of whom were Negro), and the fiasco of Little Rock under the agitation of Governor Faubus brought to a head the rise of the new South which had been latent for some years. I had left the U.S.A. for Switzerland in May, 1956, and felt as though the three years' absence from the country turned me into a stranger once again for I could not help sensing something of an electrifying tension in the air as I walked into those southern cities. Militancy was mounting on both sides of the camp although at that moment nothing spectacular was going on at any place. Revolving around the school desegregation issue, state governments were trying to find ways to let themselves off the hook with as little desegregation as possible (soon come to be known as tokenism), while the leadership of the Negro community was making it crystal clear that nothing less than full desegregation would be acceptable to them. Within the white community there was the stiffening-of-the-back of the die-hards on one hand and on the other hand the growing movement toward the acceptance of the desegregation of schools among those whose consciences were disturbed and in some instances whose pocketbooks were hurt. The South was astir although there was not a sign on the horizon that anything like a sit-in demonstration or freedom-ride was in the offing.

In this sort of an atmosphere I heard Negro leaders in city after city saying that the time had come for them to take the initiative in the movement to achieve racial justice in the South. They said in effect: We are fully aware that not all white people in the South are members or even sympathizers of the White Citizens Council. On the contrary, we know there are men and women among them who are truly Christian and are fully committed to the cause of racial justice. We also know that this is not their hour. They cannot take the initiative—and we do not expect them nor want them to do so—in any organized effort to achieve our common objectives, for the moment they stick their necks out they will instantly find themselves under organized attack, harrassment and abuse by the White Citizens Council. What good will this do for the South? If, however, the Negro leaders take the initiative we know there are increasingly large numbers of white people who will rise up to cooperate with us. Desegregation of the schools is only a tiny part of what we are aiming to achieve, and the whole thing cannot be achieved either by the white people alone or by us alone but only by cooperation of the two. In this cooperative enterprise we are the ones who must make the first move. Heretofore we have been afraid to move for we were not sure how far we could count on the white people, but now we know. And now we are ready to move.

One can see both a close similarity and a marked contrast between the statement of the Southern Rhodesian pastors and that of the Negro leaders in the U.S. South. Both are saying that they themselves must be responsible for their own destiny and must move now in a decisive way. But the one has no confidence that white colleagues will remain loyal to them at the final showdown, while the other is confident that there are white people now unseen who will rise up and fight with them.

Trends Among the Masses of Colored Races

So far I have reported only on the views expressed by a select number of highly mature leaders among the Africans in Southern Rhodesia and the Negro citizens in the southern U.S. These people are surrounded by masses of people who are looking up to them for leadership in the movement to free them from the yoke of colonialism and the vestiges of slavery. In both cases the masses are far less tolerant of the white people than their leaders are. There is, quite understandably too, a growing racism on their part against the white people both within the U.S.A. and throughout the world. One of the most extreme instances of this anti-white racism on the part of the colored races in the U.S.A. is the Black Muslim Movement. A similar trend is now seen among the younger generation of the urbanized American Indians, too.

What these people are saying is, in my opinion, twofold: In the first place, they say in effect: We have been given a raw deal for much too long a period and there is no sign that our oppressors are changing their attitude toward us. It is, therefore, up to us to change the pattern. "Eye for an eye; tooth for a tooth!" In the interest of justice we will hit back at them. Hatred for hatred, discrimination for discrimination. There will be nothing that we will do to them which they have not done to us. Ours is hatred bred by hatred, injustice to counter injustice, and, therefore, a means for the ultimate justice. We have endured humiliation long enough and are no longer willing to turn the other cheek, but stand ready to strike back.

Thus in their thinking the white man's racism against the people of colored races is a gross injustice while in the colored man's counter-racism against the white man there is a measure of justice. This makes them even more belligerent and uncompromising. Such an unequivocal and clear-cut stand is more likely to gain a mass following than a more rational and balanced stand.

In the second place, they are also saying: On the basis of their past performance we cannot believe in the integrity of white Christians. They say one thing but do another. They promise us all sorts of things but never put them into practice. We, therefore, *cannot* and *will not* believe them any more. We have been taken in by them far too often. Conferences, consultations, pronouncements, resolutions, policy statements and principles of practices, sermons, exhortations, instructions, and prayers—literally millions of words have been uttered by the churches and Christian leaders in support of equality, fair play, justice and mercy among all races, but to date our plight has hardly been improved. We can no longer take the white Christians at their word. Neither can we afford to wait for them to restore their moral integrity. Time is too short for that. We must act and act now and force them to mend their ways.

The existence of these rabid racists among the people of colored races is an indication that the masses of colored people have cast the vote of nonconfidence in the Christian leadership among the white people. Unfortunately, growing numbers of Christian people of colored races are found among those who would unabashedly vote "nonconfidence" in the ecclesiastical leadership of the Christian church in general. Those who have ears to hear cannot but hear this message transmitted all over on their faces or in the tone of their voices as an increasing number of Christians—Negro, American Indian and other ethnic groups in the U.S.A.; or Africans in Africa—meet, speak to, or talk about white Christians.

Racism—a Christian Concern

This concerns me and should concern every Christian. It should concern every Christian whether he be a white man, a Negro, an American Indian, an African, an Asian, or whatever else he may be. Not to trust other Christians and not to be trusted by them is for a Christian little short of receiving a death sentence. If the church has in any way and to any degree been responsible for the Negro Christian's loss of confidence in the white Christians or in the leadership of the church in general, the church must immediately do everything in her power to regain the Negro Christian's confidence. Otherwise the church is bound to lose her own soul, however successful and prosperous she may be in every other way. Such is the crisis of the church—not of the white race, but equally of white and Negro Christians and those of other backgrounds. When the church is under judgment no Christian can escape it. What is at stake, then, is not the survival of the white race but the survival of the church as the church, with which the Negro Christians must be just as deeply concerned as the white Christians. (More on this point in the next chapter.)

In the meantime, we must take note of the fact that in Africa this growing scepticism about the moral integrity of the Christian church has been driving the "intellectuals" in the direction of Marxism and the masses in the direction of Islam. Islam has been making tremendous inroads into West Africa and East Africa with the simplicity of its doctrine, the precision of its practical requirements, the tolerance of its racial attitude, and its acceptance of polygamy (up to four wives to be exact). African people, unsophisticated by any sort of research and investigation, would say quite firmly: Christianity is a white man's religion; Islam is a black man's religion. Obviously there is a grain of truth in this, for Christianity, introduced to them by white missionaries, has so far demanded that a goodly number of African customs and mores be done away with —including polygamy—whereas Islam has not. The African, therefore, naturally feels that Islam will let him remain an African whereas Christianity expects him to become something of a black European.

It is, therefore, not so much the revival of Islam that is undermining the Christian movement in Africa as the African's loss of confidence in the integrity of Christian leadership (which so far has remained almost exclusively in the hands of the "Europeans") that has turned him to Islam. Likewise in the U.S.A. the Black Muslim Movement is not primarily a religious movement but a protest movement against the white man who is categorically identified as Christian. What is significant in this movement is that it has chosen for its title "Black Muslims," by which militant racism and total loss of faith in Christianity are eloquently conveyed.

The most unfortunate thing about all this is that it has taken this kind of anti-white, anti-Christian movement to bring the people of Negro racial background in Africa and the U.S.A. closer together. The missionary movement of the last century and the first part of this century has not so far been able to do this. The scarcity of Negro missionaries sent out to Africa by the major denominations in the U.S.A. is very indicative. Unwittingly the missionary forces sent out by the U.S. churches confirmed the image of Christianity widely spread among African people—the religion of the white race.

Dynamics of Racism

Today in Africa and throughout the world members of colored races are being united. It is wishful to think that they are not necessarily united against the white race, for quite frankly they are. The element of counter-racism is very strong. General Carlos Romulo of the Philippines, one of the most outspokenly pro-West Asian leaders, said at the Bandung Conference, "We belong to the community of the hurt, the heart-broken and of deferred hope."[2] To be sure Bandung 1955 and a subsequent series of conferences of Afro-Asian nations have not openly declared "racial war" against the West. However, the racial feeling is one of the strongest

[2] *The Christian Century,* May 11, 1955.

factors that keeps the otherwise precarious solidarity among Afro-Asian nations from breaking down completely.

I remember an astonishing conversation I had once with a young Indonesian student in Holland. He introduced himself to me first in English and then, in perfect Japanese, spoke of how profoundly grateful he and his generation of Indonesian people are to Japan for having liberated them from the yoke of Dutch colonial imperialism. I was taken aback—in fact, quite embarrassed—and asked him how he had learned Japanese so well, thinking that by reminding him of the circumstances under which he was forced to learn Japanese I might have him qualify his statement. He got my message immediately and said: "It is true that we suffered under the Japanese occupation, but that can now be forgotten. What we cannot forget is that the Japanese have demonstrated to us that we Asians can be just as good as Europeans. For generations we had accepted as gospel truth the proposition that we were inferior to the Europeans. We had justified in our own minds our subservient position to the Dutch in our own lands. It has taken the Japanese invasion to wake us up to the fact that we can be just as good and strong as the European. For this we are eternally grateful to Japan." And to intensify my sense of embarrassment he turned to an Indian student and a Pakistani student standing near us and said to them, "You, too, must be thankful to Japan for what she has done for all of us." Subsequently I met a number of Asian students studying in European universities and among them all there seemed to exist the same feeling to a greater or a lesser degree, with the notable exception of the Korean students.

On the African scene a similar phenomenon is seen among several ethnic groups, especially in British Central Africa and the Republic of South Africa. Until recently there had been little communication let alone alignment between the African, the Colored (Euro-African), and the Asian groups. In South Africa each constitutes a separate racial category and marriages across the borders are prohibited by law. In the Rhodesias the legal restrictions are not as articulate and severe as in South Africa but in practice there is not much difference. The only conspicuous difference I noticed is that in the Rhodesias the Colored and the Asian children attend the same school, which in South Africa is prohibited. Asians in Africa are predominantly Indians and they have been treated as aliens, and religiously and culturally they certainly are alien in Africa. The colonial governments, however, seem to have placed the Asian somewhere between the European (white) and the African (black) and the underlying racist logic put them in more or less the same class as the Euro-African.

In the past the Asians in Africa used to be too proud of their cultural heritage to associate with the Africans. The Colored likewise have been told by the colonial government, not explicitly but by implication, that they were superior to the Africans because of their white blood, and they used to have hopes of being given preferential treatment by the powers-that-be in terms of appointment to civil service, etc. Having been abandoned by their white fathers, most of them were brought up by their African mothers in their grandparents' homes, but as they grew older they felt superior to Africans and tended to dissociate themselves from their families and their friends.

Of late, however, both the Asian and the Colored have awakened to the emptiness of their supposed superiority to the African and to the stubbornness with which the white people refuse to accept them as their equals. In short both the Asian and the Colored are so thoroughly disillusioned with the white leadership in politics that they are throwing their lot in the African nationalist movement, with the African people—to the consternation of the white people, I may add.

To sum up, there is afoot a militant racism all over the world that is uniting the members of colored races against the members of the white race in retaliation to the white man's past discrimination against them. This racial solidarity or alignment among colored peoples tends to take on an anti-Christian note. Christians must take the phenomenon seriously not as a threat to the white race or any other race, but as a threat to the ultimate unity of mankind and the world peace, and even more, as a threat to the integrity of the Christian church. We must, by God's grace, squarely look at this phenomenon—racism and counter-racism of this generation—not as members of any particular race but as members of the One, Holy, Catholic and Apostolic Church, in which all are bound together by their common loyalty to the Risen Christ.

CHAPTER 2

Judgment upon the Household of Faith

Conversations with Grass-Roots African Nationalists

Once I had an opportunity to pay a visit to a hot-bed of the African nationalist movement in the Luapula country of Northern Rhodesia. Prior to this visit I had met Mr. Kenneth Kaunda, national president of the United National Independent Party (UNIP), and several leaders of the same party in the Copperbelt towns. Now I wanted to meet some of the leaders in the rural areas. Not having too much time at my disposal I entrusted myself to a young African pre-medical student whom I had the good fortune to meet by chance during my stay at the Mindolo Ecumenical Center just outside the city of Kitwe, Northern Rhodesia. Let me call him by a pseudonym, Mat.

Mat chose Fort Roseberry as the place of my visit for a period of three days. It is the seat of the Provincial Government and the District Commissioner—a town that grew as an administrative center of that province with no particular industry. Outside of the township separated by a natural stream is an African location and a few miles into the hinterland is an old village. It is there that the UNIP headquarters of the northern province is located.

In the township are two hotels. Since September 1, 1960, all the hotels and restaurants in Northern Rhodesia have been desegregated by ordinance. One, however, is traditionally a European hotel and the other an African. Mat assured me that I could stay at the European hotel with no difficulty and probably as my companion he would have no trouble staying there either, but if I wanted to meet the real African leaders they would not come anywhere near me should I stay there. This left me with no choice. Mat and I took a room (a suite it was called) at the African hotel—the room No. 1, reserved for an occasional European guest, right next to the proprietor's apartment. The room faced a courtyard of green lawn on which were tables and chairs for an outdoor cafe. When the sun went down the African people flocked to this place for refreshments and chats, card games, and so forth, to enjoy the cool of the evening. I also learned that the CID (Criminal Investigation Department) policemen were always among the crowd evesdropping on the conversation among them. A few blocks from the hotel at the border between the township and the African location was a fenced-in lot used by the Public Works Department. In this lot there were two dozen or more land-rovers which I was told were armed. They were there just in case of a riot, Mat told me.

A young African trader, a personal friend of Mat's, obligingly drove us to the UNIP headquarters. The headquarters were in a mud hut with thatched roof divided into several rooms. There were no less than twenty young men and a few girls there. After waiting for five or ten minutes outside, Mat and I were ushered into the office of the provincial chairman. (Names of the people I met here are to remain unmentioned for the time being. The day will soon come, I profoundly hope, when their names can be mentioned with gratitude and praise for what they have been doing at the risk of their personal safety.) The provincial chairman was surrounded by a half dozen aides. I told him that I simply wanted to learn what he and his colleagues were thinking with regard to the future of their country. I emphasized that I took pains to come here in order to listen to the voice of the voiceless. The chairman, who appeared to be a man in his middle thirties, listened to me attentively and when I finished, he said, after a pause, "We shall take this under advisement. You will receive our answer by the end of the day." I thanked him and shook hands with everybody present and went out into the blazing sun again.

Mat and I went to the European hotel for our dinner, which we enjoyed heartily. I was gratified to note that they served the African and Asian with no fuss whatsoever. Shortly after we returned to our hotel room we heard a knock on our door. Two young men from the UNIP were there to give me their reply. We invited them in and they apologized for coming to see us so late but, they said, they had to come after dark for security reasons. Then they proceeded to tell me that they had decided to meet with me in my hotel room—again for security reasons—after dark the following night. One of them then said to Mat: "Tomorrow morning promptly at nine o'clock will you come with your companion to the UNIP headquarters? I will post a young man there to meet you and bring you to my home where I would like to have a little social get-together with you two and a small group of my personal friends–no business talk but an informal chat with this foreign guest. Will you come?" We immediately accepted, and the two emissaries disappeared into the darkness.

In the morning Mat and I walked to the UNIP headquarters, which was some little distance from our hotel. We managed to get there at the appointed hour and there was a young man waiting for us. At the host's home were five men and their wives with heaps of sandwiches, soft drinks and tea. They were all in their twenties or early thirties–youthful, attractive, and keen-looking. The men turned out to be officers of the UNIP (President, Vice-President, Secretary, Treasurer, and Program Chairman). The women did not speak or understand English very well so that one of the men had to interpret for me. When they understood my questions the women had just as much to say as the men did. They may not speak English but they are full of ideas just the same. In the course of our conversation the oldest member of the group who also was the provincial chairman of the UNIP repeatedly remarked: This is the first time for a European or a white man to walk to one of our homes and receive our hospitality and listen to what we have to say. Each time Mat corrected him that I was neither a European nor a white man and the group burst out into good-natured laughter. In the course of the morning these men and women let their hair down and literally unburdened themselves to me. Much of their pent-up emotions, grievances against white settlers, indignation against the Provincial and District Commissioners and their staff, the humiliation to which African people have been subjected all these years, their economic plight, the racial discrimination against them in every sphere of life in their own land, ruthless exploitation of the natural and human resources by the Europeans, hypocrisy of the churches and missions, various types of injustices built into the political structure of the Federation and the Protectorate government, etc., etc.—all rushed out of their mouths like a torrent for three consecutive hours. It was providential for me that we had to take time to interpret for the women every time I asked a question, as this gave me time to take notes on what they were telling me.

When noon-time came they rose and gave me a truly African farewell. We formed a circle, joined hands and they sang the anthem of the UNIP in Bemba. I of course could not understand what it said, but what a beautiful melody and what a wonderful harmony! Even without knowing one word I could sense the exuberance of their spirit and was deeply touched by it. After the singing the women bade us good-bye in the house and the men walked with us to the stream that divided the township and the African village and location.[1]

As we were walking down to the stream I saw many young children of school age curiously looking at me. I said "hello" to them a few times but there was no response. Mat whispered to me: "Say 'freedom,' and see what happens." So I shouted to the children "freedom," and instantly all the children like one mighty army shouted back, "Now," with a big smile all over their faces. But why are these children not in schools? Are there not schools they can attend? The fact of the matter is that there is no school

[1] African location is an area in an urban situation set aside exclusively for African habitation.

for them to attend save the mission school which cannot accommodate all the school age children. Many of the men active in the UNIP used to be school teachers, which in this part of the world means that they were educated in mission schools, but because of their active involvement in politics have been discharged from their posts and put on the government's black list and consequently cannot be gainfully employed. They, therefore, spend every waking hour of their life politicking. They also want to help train younger generations and wish to teach them the three R's by organizing voluntary schools. To teach children without a license, however, is a violation of the educational law; but there is not a ghost of a chance for these men to be licensed by the protectorate government to teach. What a tragic waste of human resources this is! The point was to be more sharply driven home to me during the evening of that day.

1340937

Conversations in Another Setting

As far as I was concerned I thought that during the three hours of their so-called "social" gathering all that could be learned was learned, and the evening meeting would be nothing more than a rehash of what I had already heard. Mat, however, assured me that we were going to have a lot of fun discussing strategies for the future operation of the UNIP. At any rate we were in no position to cancel the meeting. When evening came excitement began long before the meeting itself got under way. Shortly before the meeting was called to order two CID policemen (both of them African) walked into the room uninvited, which naturally caused quite a commotion. The chairman sharply rebuked the policeman by saying, "You put us all to shame by violating the basic African principle of courtesy to strangers. How dare you walk into this gentleman's private room uninvited? To crash into our meeting is one thing; to walk into somebody else's private room uninvited is quite another thing. If you are curious about our meeting, why didn't you ask for permission to come in? We are not afraid of you, neither do we have anything to hide from you. What do you think you are?" That was quite a speech. The two men did not apologize nor show any sign of going out. They just sat there. The consensus of the group apparently was that they should be allowed to stay if they wanted. So they did.

While the commotion was going on I was busy studying people. It did not take any expert to see the marked difference in calibre and character between the men I spent the morning with and the two CID policemen. The UNIP men's faces are radiant, their eyes sparkling with the singleness of their mind, purposefulness of their will, and their sense of dedication to the cause of their nation's independence and freedom of their countrymen. The CID men's faces betrayed their double-mindedness: they have families to support and to work for the government is one form of honorable industry. And yet the job consists largely of spying on their neighbors and friends and reporting on them to the authorities who in the eyes of their compatriots are nothing but agents of a foreign power! But the tragedy of tragedies is the fact that the office of the District Commissioner, on whom the Governor of the Protectorate has to depend for the local administration of law and order, is not in direct communication with the most intelligent, articulate, and dedicated group of Africans but seemingly is doing everything to alienate them. Leaders whom the Africans trust and look up to, having been thus alienated from the power structure of the Protectorate government, have gone underground. This leaves the offices of the District and the Provincial Commissioners in a state of anxiety and fear.

As I was musing on the tragicomedy of the situation unfolded before my eyes, an even more exciting thing was slowly getting under way. With the CID present among them in the persons of these two policemen, the UNIP members decided that they would not discuss politics at all. The chairman, having extended a cordial welcome to me into their midst, asked me to tell the group what my mission was, what the World Council of Churches stood for, and what I expected from this meeting. Amazingly enough this meeting turned out to be one of the most theologically profound discussions I had had in Africa or anywhere else up to this time.

I explained briefly how the World Council of Churches had come into being, going back to the origin of the ecumenical thrust inherent in the foreign missionary movement of the nineteenth century, and stated the concern of the Council for the problem of justice everywhere in the world —political, social, and economic, among which not the least is racial justice. I then said that I came to hear from them the voice which would have otherwise been left unheard. The Federal Government (then of Sir Roy Welensky) has its organ of public relations, the Protectorate Government speaks through its official channels, the United Federal Party, the Copper Mining Industry, and other Europeans' organizations publish their views and positions far and wide. I did not need to come all the way to Africa to know what they were thinking. What I hoped from a group like this was to let me hear what is closest to the heart of every African man, woman, and child.

When the meeting was opened for questions, one after another was directed to various parts of my remarks. Soon the discussion, in which most of the people, including the two policemen and the non-English speaking women actively participated, was centered on the discrepancy between the position on race relations taken by the World Council of Churches and articulated in the Evanston Statement,[2] and the practices of the Europeans in this part of Africa, beginning with the missionaries and not excluding the government officials. What good does it do, they said, for the World Council to issue such high-sounding principles if the churches and missions out here continued to behave the way they have been behaving up to now? They could and did illustrate what they meant by citing all sorts of incidents from their own experiences.

As I listened to them several things became clear to me which we have to accept as the "given" factors in this part of the world. They are:

[2] The Second Assembly of the World Council of Churches held at Evanston, Illinois, U.S.A., August 15-31, 1954, stated in one of its resolutions:
"The Second Assembly of the World Council of Churches declares its conviction that any form of segregation based on race, color, or ethnic origin is contrary to the gospel, and is incompatible with the Christian doctrine of man and with the nature of the Church of Christ. The Assembly urges the Churches within its membership to renounce all forms of segregation or discrimination and to work for their abolition within their own life and within society."

1. Missionaries are missionaries and always European, meaning white people regardless whether they are from Britain, Scandinavia, Western Europe, U.S.A., Canada, Australia, or New Zealand, and irrespective of the denominational or confessional differences of their mission boards.

2. All Europeans are assumed to be Christians by African people, whatever they may be—civil servants connected with colonial (or in the case of Northern Rhodesia, Protectorate) government, engineers or executives of the industry of an overseas company, the settler farmers, the professional missionaries—are all assumed to be Christian, and for what one of them does all are likely to be blamed.

3. Christianity is, by the African's definition, the religion of the Europeans, i.e., the white men. The value of Christianity to Africans is measured by the expressed attitude of white people among the Africans toward them. It is at this point that the church is hurt by the discrepancy between the Christian position on race relations as articulated in such documents as the Evanston Statement, and the treatment the African people receive from the Europeans living among them.

Anybody who represents the Christian church is left completely defenseless in such a discussion. There were moments when I felt I was completely licked, or the gospel itself was defeated, but toward the end of the evening the chairman spoke openly and frankly: From the way we have been criticizing the churches, the missions, and the missionaries, you might think we are anti-Christian and anti-European. I want you to know that we are neither. We are not anti-this or anti-that, except we are anti-wrong and anti-injustice. We are still Christians at heart, and want to continue to be. We are against the churches, the missions, and the missionaries because they act contrary to what we believe is the heart of the Christian gospel. When we criticize them we are doing so not as African nationalists but as Christians. I want you to understand, Mr. Kitagawa, that we are not trying to chase all the white people out of this country. We are not that foolish. We know that we need their help, their skills and their capital, and the country is large enough for them and for us. All we ask of them, and in fact the only thing we ask of them is that they treat us as grown-up human beings—nothing more but nothing less. If they do so they are not only welcome to stay among us, but they will be positively wanted by us. If, however, they will not treat us as their equals we are not going to put up with them much longer.

Christians, Churches, and Missions Under Judgment

Here the issue is not what the gospel teaches or what the church's position is with regard to race relations but how those identified as Christians are treating the African people in their daily life—in the government office, in industrial relations, across the counters of shops and stores, in restaurants, in schools and churches, in market places, and on the motor roads. Needless to say we in the U.S.A. have to bear the responsibility for many practices of Europeans thousands of miles away from us, over whom we can have no control whatsoever. The reverse is also true in that the Europeans in Africa are blamed by the Africans for our "Little Rock," "Ole Miss," and the like. Whether we like it or not we have to reconcile ourselves to the fact of contemporary life, namely that we are all in this business together. There can be no more distinction between home and overseas, the new world and the old world, North and South, down the line. Our world is one world and that is all there is to it. Christians should be the first ones to acknowledge it and accept it, but it is the Christians who are now being judged for their lack of perception of this elemental fact of life.

After everybody went home that night I continued to meditate on that day's experience. Suddenly it occurred to me that as we Christians and the churches and missions were being relentlessly criticized by those young African people, the triumph of the gospel of Jesus Christ was being heralded, for those African men and women would not have been able to criticize the churches, missions, and missionaries in the way they did, had it not been for the gospel which they had heard, received, and accepted. Had it not been for the gospel they would not have aspired to be, and be treated as, grown-up men with self-respect and dignity in relation to people from overseas with different cultures, different languages, and above all superior technology, skills, and capital with which to develop the raw and untamed country. We must face up to the fact that the Africans are now standing up against the Europeans, stating their grievances in the European languages, complaining about the mistreatment they are receiving from the Europeans, according to the moral standard of Europe which they had learned and adopted. When they complain that their human dignity is not respected by the Europeans, the gospel itself is speaking through their mouths. Their criticism of the Christian institutions is by the standard of the gospel and not anything else. The gospel is too much alive in them to permit them to condone the flagrant contradiction between the church's pronouncement and the church's practice in the area of race relations. And we must accept their criticism in humility and with penitence. To do any less is to go from bad to worse.

One of the simplest but the hardest lessons for us to learn is that the gospel we preach to others is also the standard by which we ourselves are judged. The gospel when accepted transforms him who accepts it. Often the preacher of the gospel, having delivered the gospel to others, fails to note what it has done to those persons who have accepted it. Such indeed seems to be the case with the Europeans in Africa, not the least the missionaries, in relation to the African converts. Not only do the Africans take the good news of the universal brotherhood of men at its face value, as indeed they should and have every right and obligation to do, but, more important, the gospel once accepted by a man makes a new man of him regardless of whether he is rich or poor, educated or illiterate, sophisticated or simple-minded. He becomes aware of who he is and what he is, not in terms of the human scale of values but of the divine. Though his social status may remain unchanged, his wealth does not increase and the color of his skin stays the same; he no longer feels subservient to any human being. He can look straight into the eyes of the kings, governors, employers, teachers, chiefs, or strangers without fear or embarrassment. I have seen men and women in that remote part of Northern Rhodesia doing just that—among those whom the Protectorate government had put on the blacklist on the basis of their involvement in nationalist movement. When recovered from the initial shock caused by the blow of their theologically astute and straightforward criticisms of the organized institutions of Christianity, I penitently confessed the sins of the church of which I am an integral part and praised God for the triumph of the gospel which had caught hold of the African people in spite of the churches' and missions' betrayal of that gospel.

But why, one may ask, have they left their churches, if they are as Christian as this report might indicate that they are? Why have they not stayed in their churches to reform them from within? The first thing I would like to say in reference to these questions is what you or I might have done under similar circumstances. I would not be at all surprised if we would have been far less tolerant of the shortcomings of our churches than those African brethren were of their missions. Having said this much, however, I feel constrained to add a few more remarks relating to the issue before us. For this I turn to my notes on the series of conversations I had with the African pastors and school teachers in Bulawayo, Southern Rhodesia.

Call for Contrition, Penitence, and Repentance

It was during my second visit to Central Africa (which took place in May-June, 1961) that I told a group of African pastors that I had been severely critized by the missionaries for the report I made on my previous visit. I had been told that I was much too gullible in swallowing everything the African people said about the missionaries and unduly harsh on the missionaries and other Europeans in Africa (Chapter 1). Thereupon one after another narrated to me instance after instance from their own personal experience which more than substantiated the criticisms made of the churches and missions by the UNIP people at Fort Roseberry. One told me of a mission school headmaster who would never have African members of his teaching staff into his parlor for tea, but always in the kitchen with his servants. Another one told of his missionary colleague who invited him to have tea in his garage while he and his wife were having tea in their living room. There are countless instances of African Christians from West Africa on tour who attended the "colonial" churches on Sunday and received unmistakable cold shoulders if they were not refused entrance. (One must realize that for West Africans to attend the vernacular services of African churches in East, Central, or Southern Africa is just about the same as an American attending church services completely conducted in French or in Japanese.) There are increasing numbers of African laymen who, having studied overseas, upon returning to their homelands were met by something nearing an open hostility on the part of their former teachers in mission schools for the simple reason that they behaved as though they were in no wise inferior (as indeed they were not) to the white people! All these incidents are immediately and widely known and the only conclusion that can be logically reached is that the Europeans, including the missionaries, want the Africans to learn their religion and their way of life—but only to a point. This is more than enough to drive any self-respecting African person out of the churches. The wonder is that so many of them have *not* forsaken the gospel along with the churches.

When I talked with the Europeans in Africa on the same subject, they would invariably say: Don't misunderstand us. Unlike the people of the U.S.A., we here do not have race prejudice. With us, race is not a problem at all but the crux of the matter is culture or social class. Even back home we would not think of inviting street cleaners, garbage collectors, or ordinary working class people into our parlor for tea, even though they are all white. So you see we are not keeping ourselves separate from Africans on account of their race but simply because of the cultural and social differences between us. Why, we would not know what to talk about with them if they came. These things are said by ever so many Europeans in all parts of Africa while there are emerging African men and women who have been better educated, more widely traveled and more highly cultured then they are. To those who use an argument such as is cited above, an African is categorically inferior culturally or socially. It is on this basic, unexamined assumption that such an argument is convincing to them, and this is precisely what we call race prejudice.

One finds many an exception, of course. But this is no time for us to pick out a few notable exceptions, talk them up as shining examples and congratulate ourselves for the wonderful work *they* are doing. The more Christian thing for us to do is to examine ourselves—whether we are not doing in our own situation what the African people are so rightly objecting to in their situation. As far as I can tell the Europeans in Africa, regardless of their profession or even nationalities, are made up of pretty much the same stuff as you and I. There is no assurance that we would not behave exactly the same way if placed in their situation. Indeed there is a sense in which we all share in the same guilt regardless of which race we may belong to.

The most frightful thing is that when prejudice is so completely assimilated into one's cultural upbringing, and discrimination has been built into the social structure itself, one loses sooner or later (and usually much sooner than one thinks) the capacity to sense or perceive the feelings of the oppressed—how deeply hurt they feel when they are rejected simply because of their race, color, religion, or even social status. One is likely to dismiss it by saying: Oh, I did not mean to offend them. You know I don't have race prejudice. Why should they be so sensitive about it? Those who profess to be Christians, however, are obliged to go much further. We may not have meant to hurt anybody, but if our attitude, behavior, or act hurts anybody no matter how unwittingly, we must relentlessly examine ourselves, repent and confess it.

This problem is not merely personal. To be civilized or cultured means, among other things, to have learned how to discriminate between what is beneficial and what is detrimental, and do so more or less habitually. At the same time one needs to be reminded that not to have been aware does not exonerate one from guilt. I suspect that we all have betrayed the gospel in the name of our civilization and culture—the former we preach so vehemently to the pagans to accept and the latter we cherish so dearly for ourselves that we are jealous of too many others sharing in it. When we try to accomplish both in the same place at the same time the path is bound to be narrow and slippery. The gospel can be betrayed more by well-mannered, elegantly cultured, genteel Christian ladies and gentlemen, without their ever meaning to do so, than by willful acts of raw, rugged, and wicked criminals who have no use for the church. On the matter of race I am compelled to conclude that all over the world many of us who belong to the more civilized and polite societies have been and continue to be more responsible for the perpetuation of racial discrimination than the out-and-out racists. And the damnable thing is that we do not know it nor do we want to know it.

Thus it is frequently for our complacency about and indifference to the racial issues in our society and in our churches that we are judged by the gospel in which we profess to believe and which we take the trouble of sending missionaries to preach among people of all races the world over. The real issue before us is not merely whether we ourselves are nice and kind to people of other races but how people of other races are feeling toward the race to which we belong. That you do not discriminate against nor are prejudiced against people of other races is not the end of your responsibility as a Christian. As long as there are people within your race who discriminate against people of other racial backgrounds, making them feel humiliated or rejected and consequently resentful toward your group, even though you yourself may be free from race prejudice, you as a Christian are called upon penitently to share the guilt of your race as a whole. Herein is the true repentance, which is precisely what Jesus meant when he said:

"So if you are offering your gift at the altar, and there remember that your brother has something against you, leave your gift there before the altar and go; first be reconciled to your brother. . . ." (Matt. 5:23 ff).

CHAPTER 3

The Problem of Good People Everywhere

The so-called "race problem" is in the final analysis a problem of basically good people everywhere in the world. This is a conclusion that I have personally reached after nearly two decades of involvement in race relations work in the U.S.A. and elsewhere.

Otherwise Good People

There are two aspects to what I am saying. On one hand, there are "racists" in every racial group—that is, people with strong racial prejudice, extremists, segregationists. With few exceptions these are the otherwise basically good people. Among the racists there are, of course, some criminally minded people who are trying to capitalize on good people's prejudices. But, by and large, these people—in contexts other than racial issues—are more often than not charming people, courteous, hospitable, and decent.

On the other hand, there are those people—a predominant majority of the world population—who are relatively free from prejudice (I say *relatively* free advisedly, for no one is completely free from any sort of prejudices), at least from a flagrant sort of racial prejudice, and who have not made themselves conspicuous in the area of race relations; they are the bulk of law-abiding, decent citizens who live "minding their own business." It is these people who are in the last resort responsible for many of the social troubles which seem to characterize our age. What matters here, it may be said, is a sin of omission rather than of commission.

Why then are so many of these so-called good people so hopelessly prejudiced on matters pertaining to race, and why are others who are equally good so hopelessly unconcerned about eliminating this cancerous problem from our society? In short, what is wrong with our *good* people? Here I am talking about you and me, our parents, spouses, children, brothers and sisters, neighbors, co-workers, friends and foes, their relatives and their acquaintances—in other words, everybody, literally everybody we can think of. I am not talking about mankind in general or man in the abstract but men and women of flesh and bone, living in human society, needing to love and to be loved, fearful of losing what is precious to them, often frustrated by not being able to have what they want and trying to put the blame on others for their own ills, misfortunes, and wrongs. I don't want you to lose sight of this as you read about people who are living in a remote continent or people who belong to races other than your own.

Racial Tensions, Copperbelt, Northern Rhodesia

Northern Rhodesia is a British Protectorate which along with Southern Rhodesia (British Colony) and Nyasaland (British Protectorate) constituted a territory of the British Central African Federation.[1] It is well known that the Afri-

[1] The Federation was dissolved on December 31, 1963.

can people in all three territories have always been decidedly opposed to the Federation since its formation, on the ground that the Federation was forced on them against their will, ostensibly in the interest of the balanced economic development of the three territories. Northern Rhodesia has the richest resources with its copper mines and attracts African workers from all over Africa. Notwithstanding the official slogan of the Federal Government, partnership between the racial groups, Africans were afraid that the Federation was nothing but a clever device by which Europeans in Southern Rhodesia exploit the rich resources of Northern Rhodesia and enforce the Southern Rhodesian pattern of white domination upon the other two territories. Federation and partnership were in fact forbidden words among the African people in the British Central Africa when I visited there in 1960 and 1961. Against this general background we shall see how people in the Copperbelt, Northern Rhodesia, who were otherwise good, decent, and hospitable, were having almost insurmountable difficulties between racial groups. The population of the Copperbelt (Northern Rhodesia only, excluding Katanga, Congo) was roughly estimated as 217,000 African, 43,000 European, and 3,000 Asian and Euro-African. The last-mentioned two groups were lumped together.

In October, 1960, the *Report of the Advisory Commission on the Review of the Constitution of Rhodesia and Nyasaland* was presented to the British Parliament by the Prime Minister (commonly referred to as the *Monckton Commission Report*) and was published for general circulation. In November, 1960, I found the people of the Copperbelt extremely *race relations* conscious. Note that they were not any more or less *race* conscious than they had been before, nor were they more so than people in other parts of Africa or of the world, for that matter. They were, however, preoccupied with the matter of *race relations.*

This distinction is important to make. Shortly before the Monckton Commission Report was published, the Northern Rhodesian Government had enacted the *Race Relations (Advisory and Conciliation) Ordinance* (September 1, 1960), a legislation to desegregate "hotels, cafes and cinema houses." Of interest to me was the fact that the public reaction to these two documents brought to a head many undercurrents of tensions and conflicts which had always existed between the different racial groups in the area.

I am not implying that there had been no acute race problem in the Copperbelt society before. On the contrary, the race problem has always been "omnipresent" there. Every problem there has had a racial undertone, while the race problem as such could not possibly be resolved apart from political, economic, and social measures. Racial discrimination has long been built into the social structure itself and racial tension internalized in the personal life of many an individual. It is thus practically impossible to single out or isolate the race problem as such from any other problems and consequently people there seem to have acquired the capacity to live with it without giving a second thought to it. For some years, therefore, peace, or what appeared to be peace, had prevailed among racial groups, occasional incidents now and then notwithstanding. The mind of the populace had been thus conditioned to be complacent about what had always been potential dynamite in their midst. The Race Relations Ordinance and the

Monckton Commission Report forced them to take a square look at themselves.

A Bipartite Community

The Copperbelt towns, though situated in the heart of what was the dark continent until a few decades ago, are modern industrial towns. David Livingstone's exploration of Central Africa was in the 1850's and copper was not discovered by the Europeans until the late 1920's. These towns would completely defy both your idea of Africa and your notion of a mining town. They look exactly like the modern suburban communities to be found in any part of the U.S.A., except for the African townships or locations adjacent to, but separated from, them.

The two, however, constitute one local community, each functionally depending upon the other, and the inhabitants regardless of their race share in prosperity and depression alike or suffer together from draught or epidemic which visit upon the area. To be sure, the Europeans are *more equal* than the Africans, but in the last analysis they all share in one and the same destiny as citizens of the same Copperbelt society. John V. Taylor and Dorothea Lehmann are absolutely right when they say: "The situation in the Copperbelt does not in fact present two separate traditional cultures existing in parallel but one emergent cosmopolitan society in which members of two races are inextricably interrelated in a variety of ways."[2]

And yet the Copperbelt is, for all practical purposes, a bipartite or biracial society, in spite of the several thousands

[2] Taylor, J. V. and Lehmann, D. A. *Christians of the Copperbelt*, p. 198. London: Student Christian Movement Press, Ltd., 1961.

of citizens of Euro-African and Asian backgrounds. As was pointed out in the last chapter, these people have recently been throwing their lot in with the African people, although they still maintain their respective group identities. This means that ethnic or nationality differences that exist within either the European or the African community are no longer vital. Africans are Africans regardless of their tribal nationalities while British, Canadian, Australian, American, German, Afrikaner are all lumped together as Europeans. These two major racial communities are *objectively* hanging together to make up one society but *subjectively* are two opposing parties. Most serious and unfortunate of all, the two communities were then not talking to each other. Each was talking loudly about the other to the known or unknown third party but seldom to or with each other.

In view of the inherent danger of this situation—and indeed there were signs of possible eruption seen here and there—the Mindolo Ecumenical Center located just outside of the African township of Kitwe invited me to help the churches and missions in the Copperbelt area to take relevant actions. I lived in two communities—one of the oldest and one of the newest of the Copperbelt towns—visiting mines, interviewing individuals of various races, attending church services and group meetings. I also conducted a series of seminars, discussion groups and consultations at the Mindolo Ecumenical Center with several occupational groups, which with the single exception of the top level mine managers' group were all bi- or multiracial. They were, severally, groups of clergy, school teachers, township councilors, personnel officers of industry, and civic leaders. Through these personal contacts with people, in their homes, in their offices, in the mines, in the stores, in schools, in groups and on the streets, I gained fresh insights into the basic goodness of them all, regardless of race, ethnic origin, or nationality background. In my experience there have been few people more hospitable to strangers than the Africans and the Afrikaners. Why they are not more hospitable to each other is therefore beyond my comprehension, although I have a sneaking suspicion that in a different context they could be just as hospitable to each other as they are now toward strangers from afar.

At the same time, I learned as I never had before: (1) that all these good people had been thoroughly conditioned —even strait-jacketed—by what one might call the collective mentality of the racial group to which they happen to belong, and (2) that in the Copperbelt, as elsewhere in Africa, the European and the African were living in two different worlds. As long as this situation continues it would be next to impossible for the European to feel how and what the African feels and vice versa, and between the twain there can be no empathy, no communication and no mutual understanding, let alone meeting of minds.

Two Different Worlds of Africans and Europeans

For example, a white man who is an unskilled worker in the mines, of whom there are many (not all white people are executives), is a humble and honest man earning wages to support his family. He does not pretend to be equal with the managers and other executive officers who sit in their offices. But the moment he finds himself faced by African people, regardless of who and what they are, his self-image turns into that of "master" or "boss" (or in Afrikaans "baas") with everything it connotes. He is emotionally unable to see a doctor, an engineer, a teacher, a clergyman, an artist, or what have you in an African person. To him an African is an African and cannot be anything else. Having no direct personal contact with varieties of African people except to have conversation with his house-boy or garden boy, the average European has no opportunity personally to know Africans who are better educated than himself. Consequently he never gives his thought to the plight of the African people—the gross injustice to which they have been unfairly subjected simply because they are African by race.

When I talked with white professional or business people they almost invariably said to me: Our situation is not bad, unlike that of South Africa, or the U.S.A. for that matter. Africans have come a long way. You should have seen them when I first saw them thirty years ago! There can be no comparison. We have really helped them and they are grateful to us. We get along with each other fine. As long as they keep their place we won't bother them and they don't bother us. If not for the "foreign agitators" we could in time have achieved a peaceful society in which we and Africans can live peacefully together. In saying this they were just as sincere as could be and I knew it. The trouble is that they did not know how the African people were feeling and there was no way for them to know it. They were completely separated from the African people. They were materially so well off that they seemed to have forgotten what it was like to be poor and to be humiliated for no other reason than being poor.

In the same town, the African people with whom I talked, clergyman, school teacher, labor organizer, politician, employee of mining industry, junior clerk in the District Commissioner's office—it really made no difference what they were—were unanimous in expressing their dissatisfaction with the prevailing state of race relations: All sorts of legal restrictions put on them, completely segregated and incomparably inferior living areas, limitation in employment opportunities, inferior schools in far smaller numbers in proportion to the population compared with the European community, different wage scales for equal work between Europeans and Africans, and so on and so forth. They could list two dozen grievances in two minutes! None of them were belligerent in their attitude. All were in fact quite reasonable people. There was not one African person who would advocate violence in retaliation against the Europeans or chase them out of the country.

The only logical conclusion I reached from these conversations was that the peaceful coexistence the Europeans were so proud of was almost entirely due to the patience of the Africans and most likely due to Africans' wisdom, too. The oppressed usually understand their oppressors infinitely better than the oppressors understand their victims. African people, understanding the Europeans living among them much better than the Europeans understand them, seem to be infinitely more tolerant and forgiving toward the Europeans than the Europeans can begin to appreciate. Thus there is a sense in which the African people have already won the ultimate victory in the conflict between races, even though the masses of them may not see it at all. The inner strength and serenity of a man like Kenneth Kaunda (national president of the United National Independent Party, now Minister of Local Government in the cabinet of the multiracial government of the Territory of Northern Rhodesia), have their source in his knowledge of this very fact. Today the apathy of the majority of Europeans toward the plight of Africans and the belligerence toward Europeans on the part of increasing numbers of less informed Africans are driving sound leaders like Mr. Kaunda among the Africans and Sir John Moffatt among the European colonists into a well-nigh impossible position. It is evident that as long as communication is not established between the two major racial communities this predicament cannot be removed.

Schoolteachers' Consultation

The lack or complete absence of communication between the two racial communities was manifestly demonstrated in the series of group discussions held at the Mindolo Ecumenical Center. I shall never forget the painful few hours I spent with a group of school teachers there. One would have thought that they being of one profession though of different races, besides being Christian, would have something in common between them and therefore could engage in conversation with one another relatively easily. My experience proved otherwise. At first each group was afraid of the government, then each was suspicious of the other, and finally they together were suspicious of me and my sponsor. I do not now, nor did I then, blame them for these suspicions. They were only indicative of the social climate in which they had been compelled to live. Taken individually, every one of them, as I vividly recall, was an attractive person, male and female, European and African alike.

European teachers taught in schools exclusively for European children, and in schools for Asian and Euro-African children, both of which were under the Ministry of Education of the Federal Government, while African teachers taught only in schools exclusively for African children, which were under the Department of Native Affairs of the Territorial Government. There were thus two sets of teachers accountable to two different school systems, with two sets of governing laws, two curricula with two sets of textbooks, educating two sets of children, all divided by racial distinction. African and European teachers furthermore were living in two different locations, with two completely different sets of neighbors and extra-professional friends and acquaintances. Add to these differences the enormous difference in their educational backgrounds and standards of training. Though both were school teachers, the two were living in two distinctly different worlds. How could the twain ever meet?

As long as they were allowed to stay within the confines of their professional concerns in the technically defined sense, conversations did not get very far. It was only when we lifted our horizons and started to discuss what sort of society was emerging in the Copperbelt and what sort of education might be required to prepare the children for that new society that a lively discussion began to take place. After two long and rather arduous days they as a group stated that as professional educators they considered it not only meaningless but positively harmful to educate children of European and African descent under two different and mutually unrelated school systems by two mutually exclusive sets of teachers, inasmuch as they were growing to be citizens of one multiracial society in which all were interdependent. Not a world-shaking resolution you would say, and I agree. It is not a whit more world-shaking than the famous Supreme Court decision of May 17, 1954, that racial segregation in public schools is unconstitutional. One significant thing about the school teachers' statement is that it was not a decision handed down by a court, but a conclusion reached by themselves after two days of soul-searching together.

As I rejoiced with what the teachers did, I could not help wondering why these good men and women had never met one another before. They all, as I recall, were Christians—not nominal but practicing, church-going Christians. Though divided into various denominations as well as between Africans and Europeans, could not the church have somehow provided opportunities for these Christian teachers to get together and share with one another their professional concerns from time to time? The church, whose leadership has been in European hands, had not thought of it as something even remotely connected to its ministry. The moaning and groaning of the African teachers just could not reach the range of hearing of the comfortably situated and well-protected leadership of the church.

Councilmen's Consultation

We had to go through the same sort of painful process with the members of the local community councils, personnel officers and even the clergy. At one of the sessions with councilmen the contrast of vantage points between the African and European became crystal clear. A couple of charming European members kept on emphasizing how raw and unlettered the African people were as they first knew them, and how with them it was not racial discrimination but discrimination based on culture or social class. They said: It has taken us four centuries to reach our present stage of civilization and it is absolutely inconceivable that these African people, so raw and primitive only thirty years ago, could now be as civilized as we are. Give them time and they will eventually be like us but it will take several generations before that day comes. Listening to these statements were several African men, intelligent, courteous, patient, and articulate. They were indeed courteous enough to let the European members finish their pieces and then quietly, gently, but nonetheless firmly and thoroughly, refuted every argument which had been used to justify the discriminatory practices. These men have their eyes fixed on the future—the tomorrow of their country, free from the yoke of colonialism. Besides, those African people who are now in the Copperbelt are completely detribalized if not fully urbanized and do not know at first hand the "raw and primitive" Africans the European members are dwelling so much on.

After one of the sessions a couple of younger European men said to me: "This is absolutely the first time for us to sit with African men who are able to talk the way these men do." The younger generation in the European group appeared to have much less to unlearn and therefore they could accept the modern African much more readily, but the older generation seemed to be utterly incapable of liberating themselves from the stereotype image of the primitive African and, therefore, unable to accept the reality of contemporary Africa. At the moment, the social climate within the European community appears to be dominated by the loudly vocalized opinion of the reactionary and unenlightened generation. On the part of the African community the generation which silently and blindly obeyed the Europeans as master or "baas" is no longer in the saddle but the forward-looking youthful men in their thirties or under. This sharp cleavage of generations between the leadership of the two racial communities makes the problem of inter-group communication extremely difficult.

Up to now the rigid separation, legal and extralegal, of the European's residence from the African's has made it humanly impossible for individual members of both communities to get to know one another on a personal or family basis. Under such circumstances there is no use exhorting European people to be nice and kind to African people and to respect their personalities, for they never have a chance to meet African men and women, whom they can love and respect, whom they can talk to and listen to, with whom they can share joys and sorrows, have debates, iron out differences of opinions on matters of common concern, and enter into genuine personal relationship. The otherwise good European Christians have kept on saying that "as soon as the Africans become worthy of our respect and friendship we shall receive them into our midst," never realizing that as long as they are kept apart they will never be able to meet among the African those who are more than their match. The churches, however they are organized, with all their shortcomings and defects, are still the best agency to provide a favorable context or framework in which people of different racial stocks can meet and converse with one another. Sadly the churches have not been doing this. On the contrary they have been afraid of doing anything of the sort.

Clergymen's Consultation

At a clergy meeting one bright and forthright young African pastor articulated the feeling which was shared by all the African pastors present when he said: "We should go back to the old pattern and have two churches—one African and one European; then we shall at least be honest with ourselves. Now, since a few years ago, we call ourselves *The United Church of Central Africa in Rhodesia,* presumably under one administration, but in reality we are still separated. When we go to the European churches we are made to feel that we are not really welcome, and that we do not really belong to the same church. If we meant business, why shouldn't we build one big enough church between the European and African townships and worship together? Do we have to wait until the civil authorities desegregate the residential areas to start worshipping together? Ought we not to take the lead in the direction of desegregation even while we are separated and a lot of hurdles are to be overcome?" All the excuses put forward by the shocked European pastors in charge of European congregations pointing out why such moves could not be made for some time to come sounded both shallow and hollow. These good parsons, well educated and properly trained, could immediately realize exactly what their congregations would feel, should such a proposal be made to them, but they could not begin to comprehend what the African Christians are *now* feeling, even while one of them is addressing himself directly to them on that very point.

Handicap of the Privileged

What is wrong with the European Christians? Are they callous? Do they really despise, if not hate, Africans? Or are they blind so that they cannot see those Africans who are as well educated as they are if not better? The main trouble with the Europeans is that they are too "privileged" to be human in their relationships with those who are underprivileged, or they have been too far removed from the actual life of the African people to maintain human contact with them. Insularity, both mental and physical, of the Europeans in the Copperbelt society, I believe, has caused them to become more and more introverted in the face of the rising movement of African nationalism throughout the continent, so that the European community has become a fear-ridden, psychopathic community filled with anxiety for the future and suspicion for the unknown, trying to assure itself of safety by making the walls surrounding it more and more impenetrable. The inevitable result is the further blocking of communication between the inside and the outside of the walls, making the community inside an ostrich-like fool's paradise.

Is this the best Christianity can do for the Europeans in the Copperbelt? Is this the kind of Christianity missionaries have been propagating among the Africans there or for that matter all over the world? Missionaries, be they Scotsmen or Englishmen, Canadian or Australian, or even German or Dutch, are there as elsewhere, just as much in the name of American churches as in others. Insofar as they and we are members of the One, Holy, Catholic, and Apostolic Church, they are *our* missionaries, and we are there with them, and we share with them the responsibility for the result of their toil—failure as well as triumph. Moreover, in the eyes of the Africans, Christians and non-Christians alike, there is no difference between Americans and Europeans, and what they hear and read about the racial strife in the U.S.A. or Britain simply confirms the impression made on them by the pathological behavior of the European community in their midst. The pioneering missionaries risked their own lives to save the souls of Africans. Europeans in today's Africa, missionaries, pastors, and others, seem to be preoccupied with saving their own skins at the expense of their own souls.

CHAPTER 4

Power Relations Between Dominant and Minority Groups in the U. S. A.

Race Relations as Primarily Inter-Group Relations

In the last chapter we have seen, by way of a case study of one specific area, how with the race problem, so-called, the trouble lies with basically good and decent people, that is, law-abiding citizens who mind their own business, and how relatively ineffective the churches and missions have been in dealing with such people in race relations. The social, political, and economic injustices, the denial of human rights, dishonoring of personal dignity, and the prevention of wholesome growth of children, etc., suffered by minority or oppressed racial groups as a result of the racial discrimination practiced against them by the majority or dominant group are unmistakably moral issues. There are no two ways about it. Discrimination against a person or a group of people on the basis of race, color, or ethnic origin is clearly immoral. But the church's failure in dealing with the racial problems lies in the fact that she has dealt with it *solely and exclusively* as a moral issue, and therefore as a primarily personal matter.

In my observation, both here in the U.S.A. and elsewhere in other lands, racial conflict is primarily an inter-*group* tension rather than inter-*personal,* and a matter of power relation rather than one of morality alone. It of course becomes an object of ethical concern not only for Christians but also for all civilized people, and it does so in pretty much the same way as does the possession of wealth, or of nuclear power. The first order of business for us as Christians, therefore, is to recognize the racial conflict for precisely what it is and to understand its dynamics so that we may know what to do with it.

Racial tensions are found all over the world today. International relations are not entirely free from racial undertones, to which I shall devote the next chapter. Few nations are without interracial conflict of one sort or another within them. In our country, where practically every state and every city is infested by this problem, Christians have been guilty either of reducing it too quickly to a moral, ergo personal, issue, or of treating it exclusively as a legal or constitutional issue, in which the U. S. Supreme Court instead of the gospel has the final word. As a corrective to this two-fold error, I propose to analyze at least three different types of power relations between the dominant and minority groups in our country, in which history plays a tremendously important role.

In the U.S.A.: Three Patterns

Roughly speaking, the U.S.A. today, as it has been for the past 200 years, is a society which consists of a complex of power relations between one dominant group and several kinds of minority groups, racial and otherwise. The one dominant group in the area of race relations is the so-called white American, namely the Anglo-European colonists and immigrants and their descendants. There are three major types of minority groups, namely: (1) *indigenous minority*—the American Indians; (2) *imported minority*—the Negro Americans; and (3) *alien minority*—the Oriental Americans (Chinese, Japanese, Filipino, etc.).

These typological adjectives are used tentatively and must not be *absolutized.*

That there might have been differences in their relationships to the dominant group on the part of these three minority groups can readily be imagined. I should like to analyze them more or less systematically.

THE INDIGENOUS MINORITY

When the first groups of colonists arrived on the Atlantic shore, the indigenous population of course far outnumbered them. But on account of its technological superiority, the incoming group soon subjugated the indigenous. The symbol of this complete reversal of status between the American Indians and the colonists is the Indian Reservation. The colonists soon assumed the role of "model-builder," and the Indians were given a choice between two alternatives: either to conform to the colonists' way of life (characterized by white man's way, English language, "Christian" civilization, etc.) and survive, or to be exterminated (either literally killed off or put away on the reservations). In this situation the initial reaction of the American Indians to the colonists could not but be resentment and hostility. The subsequent relationships between the two groups may be described as follows:

1. The superiority complex on the part of the colonists, without any respect for the culture or the value system of the American Indians, was epitomized by the saying, "The only good Indians are dead Indians." Indians were "accepted" by the whites when they *ceased* to be Indians, having adopted the white man's way, learned to speak English, and become pants-wearing Christians. Here is an unabashed expression of cultural imperialism in which the Christian missionaries had a large share.

2. Correspondingly, the inferiority complex on the part of the American Indian expressed itself as ambivalence toward the colonists' civilization. Indians, whether they liked it or not, had to recognize how powerful the colonists' civilization was. In this new situation, in which the colonists constituted the dominant group, the Indians willy-nilly had to depend on them for *survival*. They could not chase the colonists out. "If you cannot beat them, join them" became the only way left for them. Indians had to admire and resent the colonists and their civilization. The Indians' wish would have been to chase the colonists away. When that proved impossible, their second choice was to run away from the colonists, and some actually took this course. This, too, proved unsatisfactory, for even in the state of escape they had to depend on the colonists' government for bare subsistence on the reservations. Finally, therefore, they were compelled to "adopt" the white man's way against their own will and desire. Consequently, their mental attitude toward the white man's civilization has remained even to this day *basically negative*. They learn it because otherwise they cannot survive, but they know that as a result of adopting it they are forfeiting their birthright as Indians

and are turning into something other than what they were born to be.

Many so-called "Indian wars" must be seen in the light of this power relationship between the immigrant white Americans and the indigenous Americans. They were all suicidal attempts on the part of the indigenous tribes to maintain their cultural autonomy and ethnic identity in the face of the encroaching, powerful, alien civilization. And the victory of the white man never succeeded in turning the Indians' resentment into unmixed admiration of the white man's power, but only resulted in his ambivalence toward the white man and his power.

THE IMPORTED MINORITY

The Negro Americans were originally brought into North America by the Anglo-European colonists as slaves, which meant that their ethnic and cultural ties with their native lands had been completely cut off prior to their coming here. They had been reduced to a culturally uprooted (or denationalized), ethnically displaced (de-tribalized) group of people to be herded to an unknown land. The slaves then belonged neither to America nor to Africa but were private possessions of their masters. The ancestors of the Negro Americans were thus individuals who were forced to lose group-identity of every sort—cultural, ethnic, and what have you. The only thing that was common among them was the fact that they were all slaves, and there evolved a latent community, a people bound together by their common suffering and oppression. They were thus *imported* into America as something far less than a minority group, for insofar as the colonists were concerned their slaves had no status whatsoever in the society. They were simply the personal property of their masters.

By the time the Emancipation Proclamation was issued, the ex-slaves and the descendants of slaves had been to a considerable degree indigenized in the American soil, acquiring a high degree of group solidarity solely on the basis of their racial stock on the one hand, and sharing to whatever degree they were permitted in the white American's culture and civilization on the other. The tribal memberships or cultural backgrounds of their forefathers having been completely annihilated, they were simply and solely identified as Negroes. Culturally, by then, they were not very much different from white Americans.

Now, as the originally imported but since then thoroughly indigenized minority group, the Negro Americans' attitude toward the white Americans in the post-emancipation period has been characterized by the effort to restore to themselves full human dignity and gain civil rights on equal terms with the dominant group. Unlike the indigenous minority, the Negro Americans do not have any peculiar culture of their own to defend against the encroaching culture of the white people. What may be peculiarly Negro insofar as their culture goes is neither rooted in their ancestral culture in Africa nor inherent in their biological heritage as the racial group (as their pigmentation is), but stems from their collective experience of slavery, oppression, and suffering over several generations. Negro Spirituals may be taken as one of the most conspicuous expressions of this.

The struggle between the white and the Negro Americans collectively has for many years been, on the part of the Negro to gain in full what the white has, and on the part of the white, to keep the Negro from gaining one whit more than what he already has.[1] To put it bluntly, both groups belong to one and the same country, and share in one and the same national culture, except the white wants to keep the Negro down as a second-class citizen, while the Negro fights to eliminate all differences in status that are based on race. In this situation the white American would not think of making "white men" out of the Negroes as he tried to do in the case of American Indians. Any Negro person who in any sense whatsoever *ceases* to be Negro, (e.g., one who "passes" as a white) is not only unacceptable, but positively offensive, to the whites. To them the Negro has been acceptable only so long as he remains manifestly a Negro and stays "in his place." While in relation to the American Indian the white American's attitude has been dominated by the sense of superiority, in relation to the American Negro it has been dominated by the sense of anxiety. The social segregation of the Negro is most indicative of this anxiety.

In this connection one must not overlook the strong element of the collective sense of guilt on the part of the white Americans for the historical fact of slavery. The guilt will survive as long as the manifest offense remains unforgiven. This, in turn, drives the guilty to take every conceivable

[1] Lest I should be misunderstood, let me reiterate that here I am not talking about personal attitudes, or outlook of the individual person, but about what I have earlier called "collective mentality." There are many so-called "Southern whites" whose attitudes toward the Negro are completely free from this kind of preoccupation. Their struggle is how to free themselves from the collective attitude of their group toward the Negro group.

measure to keep the offended out of touch, if not completely out of sight. This is one of the cornerstones for segregation as a social institution.

Over against this, the Negro American's attitude toward the white Americans is bound to be and indeed has become increasingly more aggressive. Unlike the American Indian, whose attitude toward the white American has remained ambivalent, the Negro American now takes an unequivocally belligerent attitude toward the whites, and he will never stop short of full equality with them. His fight will continue until he gets what he is convinced is his due. This makes the white American all the more anxious, in spite of the plain fact that the Negro American is not trying to conquer white Americans, but only demanding to be treated as their equal. The white Americans tend to feel that the Negro American is trying to dominate them in retaliation for what they had subjected him to in the past. Here again one sees how deeply the sense of guilt conditions the white man's attitude toward the Negro.

THE ALIEN MINORITY

The Chinese, Japanese, and Filipinos were all brought to the Pacific shore by American industry as cheap labor. Unlike the Negro slaves these Oriental laborers were not completely uprooted from their respective countries, but rather it was insisted that they retain their ties with their own countries and come to the States only to sell their labor and return home as soon as their contracts were over. They were meant to be neither colonists nor immigrants, although they were not intended to be slaves. They were alien laborers employed by Americans for a definite period of time. The logical extremity of this outlook on the part of the Americans was the Oriental Exclusion Act of 1924.

The attitude of the Americans notwithstanding, this provided to tens of thousands of Asians the golden opportunity to migrate into the New World to improve their economic status. To be sure, a predominant majority of them came to the U.S.A. with the idea of working for a few years and then returning home with a load of money. But once they had arrived here it became perfectly clear to them that (1) they could not possibly make enough money in such a short space of time, but (2) should they stay longer and possibly be permitted to become an integral part of America, they could live an infinitely better life than they could ever hope for back in their own countries. They therefore chose to be immigrants rather than merely contract laborers. Here they were regarded by the white Americans as "the Yellow Peril," and every conceivable means was used to discourage them from becoming integrated into American society. For this purpose, even the myth of "unassimilability of the Asiatics" was created. Racial discrimination and social ostracism, threat and humiliation, restrictions, and prohibitions, legal and extralegal, if not illegal, were used to force them to remain alien, making it unmistakably clear to them that they may possibly be tolerated in America but will never be accepted.

Over against this attitude of the Americans toward them, the Oriental immigrants have persistently tried to become as fully Americanized as possible—even if they were to return to their own countries, they wanted to return home fully Americanized!

The outright rejection of the alien minority by the dominant group is matched by the minority's identification with the dominant group at any cost—almost an unconditional surrender to it! Americans attempt to keep them alien, while they attempt to Americanize themselves. They are willing to pay any price for full acceptance by the American society—for it they are even willing to sell their birthright! An example of this attitude is seen in the attitude of many Japanese Americans who used to refuse to be identified as Japanese, insisting with pathological emphasis that they were Americans and nothing else, that they could not even speak the Japanese language nor could they appreciate the Japanese arts! They were quite prepared to de-culturize themselves, if it would help them to be accepted by the majority group, which otherwise flatly rejected them.

An interesting thing about the members of this group is that, after the group is more fully accepted by the majority group and its position more securely established in the American society, they tend to revive their interest in the cultural heritage of their ethnic group. The alien minority cannot erase its ethnic peculiarity, so that even after being fully accepted, its members remain ethnically identifiable. That is to say, ethnic difference in the final analysis has nothing to do with their rejection or acceptance by the majority group. The crux of the matter is their "alienness"—while they are rejected as aliens, ethnic differences are used as a convenient alibi to reject them!—but, when they are fully accepted and cease to be alien, then their ethnic difference often becomes something of a mark of distinction, an object of curiosity (in a very healthy sense) of members of the majority group toward them, and on the whole an asset rather than a liability for them. (This is the basic difference between Oriental Americans and Negro or Indian Americans.) When the society becomes thus wholesome in its inter-group relations, the members of the ex-alien minority group would not hesitate to identify themselves with the nationality background of their group and even take pride in its cultural heritage. To put it differently, they can accept themselves as they actually are only when the majority group first accepts them as their equal and treats them accordingly.

To summarize, we have seen three different types of power relations between majority and minority groups in the U.S. society. To one and the same dominant group the three types of minority groups reacted in three different ways:

1. *Ambivalence* to the encroaching and conquering group
2. *Belligerence* to the group that had been exploiting and oppressing them
3. *Surrender* to the group that represents to them the ideal state for themselves

Minority Groups Assert Their Group Identity

Now, to complicate the problem, there is a new factor at work today just as dynamic as the history internalized as the collective attitude of several ethnic groups, namely what I have earlier called counter-racism. All the three groups mentioned above are now doing two apparently contradictory things simultaneously: (1) asserting each its own group identity and autonomy and (2) demanding full integration in the U.S. society. This is neither ambivalence nor self-contradiction on their part but is indicative of the stage at which mankind finds itself in world history at the present moment, and which forces the dominant group to rethink seriously its attitude toward these ethnic groups in its midst. Since 1954 we have been preoccupied with the issues of desegregation and integration not only in the southern states but all over the nation. What desegregation means is clear enough but what does integration mean? Too often it seems to be glibly taken for granted that ethnic groups of all sorts should give up their group integrity and their members should as individuals join the majority or the dominant group. Is this not what the "melting pot theory" means—along with its end result, which is called "assimilation"? Is this not what the white man is afraid will happen and what others are equally vehemently objecting to? No self-respecting Negro today wants to "pass." No self-respecting American Indian desires to cease being an Indian now. No self-respecting Oriental American minimizes his ethno-cultural heritage anymore. This does not mean that they all are opposed to "inter-marriage"; they have never been so eager to "inter-marry" as some pathological racial purists seem to think. That which needs to be fully recognized once and for all is that to members of various ethnic groups inter-marriage has seldom been and will never be an issue. They are neither for nor against it and never lose sleep over it as an issue. To make an issue of inter-marriage and to use it to oppose integration is to muddle the matter. It betrays the type of mentality which assumes that one's own group is so splendid that everybody else is dying to join it. If integration meant something like this, no self-respecting member of any of the ethnic groups would want it.

What then do they want? This, too, is a wrong way to put the question. It is not what either the majority or the minority groups want but what is best for both of them, or all of them, together and in relation to one another. More will be said about this in another chapter, and in the meantime it may be enough to suggest that power relations among several ethnic groups each maintaining its group integrity will be one of the crucial factors to understand what integration should mean and how it can be achieved.

To the three groups mentioned above, we now have to add the Spanish-speaking people. What their posture toward the dominant group is like requires more careful observation at this point. The U.S.A. since World War II has been much more avowedly pluralistic in its orientation to ethno-cultural problems than ever before so that one can expect a rather different type of reaction on the part of the recent in-migrant groups from beyond our southern border.

Traditional View of the Churches on Ethnic Groups in the U.S.A.

Among all these ethnic groups U.S. churches have been doing much missionary work. In terms of race or ethnic relations what have been the contributions so far made by the church? It is about time for us to ask this question. Do we, who have established and carried on Chinese and Japanese missions on the Pacific Coast, Negro missions in the south and elsewhere, Indian missions all over the reservations, and are still supporting them loyally and generously, do we have any idea what the racially integrated church is or should be like? If we don't know it, how can we talk about a racially integrated society?

How many of us, supporters of missions among these ethnic groups within our borders, know from first-hand experiences what Christian fellowship is that transcends racial and ethnic differences? To give money for missions, to support missionaries, to knit and sew for the children of missions—all these are one thing. To enter into fellowship with our fellow Christians in these missions is quite another thing. Unless and until we experience this latter relationship I do not believe we have anything unique to contribute in terms of race relations.

Our missions among ethnic groups, though within our borders, have basically been exactly the same as our foreign missions in orientation, in operative principle, and in expectation. Be they indigenous minority, imported minority, or alien minority, from the standpoint of our churches' missionary work, "they" have all been people apart from "us" who support the missions and send the missionaries out to them.

Somehow the thought has seldom occurred to us that they might some day come into our churches to share in the Christian fellowship with us not as our guests nor as exhibits of our splendid work . . . but as *part of us.* Many of us would have hesitated to support those missions, had we thought that some day we might be kneeling at the altar-rail receiving the sacraments from "one of them" as our rector, or listening to "one of them" preach as our pastor.

If such a thought makes us hesitate to support missions

among the ethnic groups within our borders, what about our moral integrity in supporting missionary work overseas? The truth of the matter is that a good many of us have been supporting missionary work among the ethnic groups within the U.S.A. as if they were "foreign people" abroad.

We have been guilty of this sub-Christian attitude toward members of various ethnic groups partly because we have never fully understood the dynamics inherent in the power-relations that existed between the dominant group and minority ethnic groups. Consequently we have failed to mention their behavior and attitude in reaction to our action, behavior, or expression of concern; we have jumped to the conclusion that these people are different from us; they would not feel comfortable with us; they would prefer to be with their own people; and we should never think of forcing them to join us, etc. In the church we do not have such a crude thing as "restrictive covenant," but have we not tacitly assumed that American Indian candidates for Holy Orders are for Indian missions, Negro seminarians are for Negro parishes, etc.? Until recently few mission boards have thought of them as potential overseas missionaries! Having thus arbitrarily restricted their potential sphere of operation, we have been complaining how few of them have presented themselves as candidates for the ministry of the church!

It is the power relations between the dominant and minority groups, not the races as such, that complicates personal relationships between individual members of those groups. To be Christian in this context means to enter into genuine, human, interpersonal relationships with people who belong to groups other than one's own. This cannot happen just by being ignorant of the power relations that do exist. Ignorance about them makes one their victim. This is precisely what has happened to the churches in the U.S.A. The operative principle of their missionary work among the Indian Americans, Negro Americans, and Oriental Americans have been perfect reflections of the general patterns of relationships between the dominant, white American group and these ethnic groups—so much so that one wonders which came first—the church's own actual attitude or that of the public which we so often deplore!

CHAPTER 5

Power Relations Between the West and Emerging Nations: Racial Undertones

Modern Missionary Movement and Expansion of the West

Today Christians are found all over the world. This is the achievement of the missionary movement of the last two centuries, which has coincided with the dynamic expansion of the West both in terms of commerce and industry and of colonial imperialism. There are some places where missions led the way, others where commerce opened the way, and still others where power politics forced the way open. Whatever the order in which they went, the missions usually helped the others and others helped the missions, so much that an indelible impression has been made upon the Afro-Asian people that Christianity is the white man's religion and Christian missions and colonial imperialism are two sides of one coin. Until World War II most of the Afro-Asian countries, few of which were then independent nations, acquiesced to the Western dominance over them, but since then their attitude toward the Christian missions from the West has become exceedingly critical. (A similar attitude can also be seen increasingly in the general area of international relations.) The West no longer enjoys "free passage" everywhere in the world as it used to. In all these strained relations between the West and Afro-Asian countries there are unmistakable racial undertones. Can this be explained as another case of counter-racism or is this something else? It is important for us to understand this because it has far reaching implications for the mission of the church in the contemporary world.

Racial Undertones in Contemporary International Relations

The racial undertones in international relations come from the historical fact that the relationships between the West and the rest of the world, and more particularly Asia and Africa, have been—as the often-used phrase "impact of the West" suggests—various types of majority-minority relationships. It must be said at this point that in no country does any particular type prevail exclusively or consistently. The power relations may change from one type to another from one period to another in one country, or more than one type may exist simultaneously in one country, or all types may be inseparably mixed up. Nevertheless typological analyses help to clarify the social dynamics that operate in the now-developing countries which have been undergoing rapid social change under the impact of the West.

Here I venture a typological hypothesis of the initial attitudes on the part of Asian and African countries to the encroaching impact of the West: (1) the countries that were more or less overrun by the West; colonialized countries such as India, Indonesia, Burma, etc., in Asia, and most countries in Africa south of the Sahara; (2) the countries that attempted to keep the West at a distance upon failing in their initial effort to keep it out completely, e.g. China; (3) the countries that positively tried to take in as much of the Western civilization as possible, or that attempted to westernize themselves as fast as possible, e.g. Japan and Turkey.

THE COLONIALIZED COUNTRIES

The term "colonialized" is used to indicate a country where Western nations colonized. These countries, at the time when the West moved in on them, were neither interested in Western civilization nor ready to adopt it. But neither were they strong enough to keep it out. In short, they were *conquered* by the Western powers to be ruled by them. The indigenous population of such a country was reduced to the status of a minority in relation to the colonial government. In Dr. D. T. Niles' characteristically polite phrase, the indigenous people became "guests" of the foreigner in their own country while the foreigner became the "host." This is precisely the same status as that of the indigenous minority in the U.S.A.

. . . *Case of India*

In India, for example, there developed a severe conflict between the Indian who tried to maintain his age-old culture and the Britisher who tried to override it with Western civilization. Owing to its superiority in technology the British colonial government was able to impose its own policy upon India. Not infrequently changes brought about by the colonial government helped improve the life of the Indian.

Once seeing such positive possibilities, the Indian could not help being attracted to the Western civilization. But to adopt it was to be conquered by it, giving up his own culture, and therefore it was extremely painful. The Christian missionaries preached Christianity as *the religion of civilization*—that of the civilized people and that which civilizes the primitive peoples. In the most profound sense, the missionaries were the greatest of all the threats from the standpoint of the Indian, for they did not merely introduce a new technology but stood for a complete re-making of the Indian man: it was his soul that they were after! They were gentlemen of genuine goodwill, unselfish and devoted to the well-being of the Indian. What they taught was noble and reasonable and therefore naturally attracted the Indian; but much more than this, the religion they preached was a threat to the Indian, for it would not stop short of his "death to his old self" (Hindu Indian) and "rebirth as a new man" (Westernized Christian). The same situation prevailed in most other countries of Southeast Asia.

What Christianity thus represented was also represented to a lesser degree by everything else of the Western civilization: Roman law, modern education, English language, medicine, plantation, factory, railroad, and all sorts of machines. Any of these things, once adopted by even a small segment of an Asian nation, has a way of causing an all-pervading change in the pattern of the national life. To change subsistence farming into a marketing agriculture may appear to be a marvelous thing—innocent enough at any rate—

but it is bound to change the whole pattern of life of the entire nation. The Indian may soon have to cease being Indian and turn out to be something entirely new!

It is painful to foresee this happening, even though the Indian can readily see all sorts of benefits connected with it. Gandhi's anti-industrialism must be seen in this light. In this situation the Southeast Asian nations' attitude toward British colonialism may be said to have been similar to that of the North American Indians toward the Anglo-European colonists—the indigenous minority versus the dominant foreigner, in which the latter imposes its own way upon the former without ever bothering to gain its consent, let alone approval.

People under the colonial domination of the Western powers are finally compelled to adopt the Western civilization as the only survival technique—to "fight the enemy with the enemy's weapon"! In North America the Indians finally *failed* in this attempt for two reasons: (1) Their civilization was too weak to withstand the technical civilization of the West, and (2) the colonists soon became independent of countries of their origin and made the New World their own country, indigenizing themselves, calling themselves Americans and soon outnumbering the aboriginal population. India and other Asian countries which had once been colonized by the Western powers succeeded in adopting the civilization of their colonial rulers to the extent that they could demand and gain political independence from the West.

This they were able to accomplish because (1) they were all countries of old and highly developed civilizations, making them capable of adapting themselves to Western civilization although it was of an extremely different type from their own and was imposed upon them against their will or desire; and (2) their countries had remained "colonies" in which the resident whites had never outnumbered the indigenous population. Englishmen might have tried to make India a second England, but they never thought of becoming Indians! That is to say, with all the attempts to impose Western civilization upon India, it was never fully "domesticated" or "naturalized" in India, but always remained "alien" to India and her people. Indians had to be "Westernized" in order to enjoy it or benefit from it, and by so doing they learned how to assert their national autonomy in relation to their colonial rulers in the latter's terms!

. . . *African Countries*

What I have been saying about India can be applied not only to other Asian countries but also to most areas in Africa, excepting that in Africa the relationship between the indigenous African and the Anglo-European population resembles more closely that of the American Indian and the white American in that there had not been any "nation" in Africa except tribal nations prior to the invasion of the West and it is the colonial powers that have been responsible for building nations in Africa. (The unique case in this respect is the Union of South Africa, in which both the African and the European are originally immigrants, both of whom today claim South Africa as their own homeland and the only country they belong to.) In Africa, south of the Sahara, the indigenous population was reduced to the status of *indigenous minority* by the Anglo-European colonizer, and in the course of developing different countries under colonial rule after the Western pattern of nation-state, much of the indigenous population has been *detribalized* and become *dispossessed.*

Those thus detribalized were the first Africans whom the Christian missions had to deal with and, in a real sense, were able to deal with. In subsequent years the missionary enterprise either prospered only after detribalization had been accomplished by some other forces, or initiated the process of detribalization as a consequence of somehow converting a few numbers out of a given tribe. The result is that the Africans were not only reduced to the status of indigenous minority but were "alienated" in their own lands, and their relationship to the Europeans in Africa became somewhat similar to a mixture of that of the American Indian and that of the Negro American to the white American in the U.S.A.—as if they had been "imported" from outside, displaced and dispossessed, rid of a culture of their own, and completely at the mercy of the European, dependence upon whom is the only condition for their survival. In this situation they have been acceptable to the European colonizer only if they adopted his culture but at the same time "stayed in their place" as designated by him.

This background of the strained relationship between the European and the African may help explain the curious mixture of two movements in Africa: (1) *nationalism* along the line of the Western concept of the politically autonomous nation-state and (2) *nativism* along the line of rejection of everything foreign with nostalgic longing to return to the primitive pattern of their ancestral culture. One is a positive adaptation to the Western civilization, while the other is a reactionary rejection of the same. In fact, African *nationalism* tends to become nativistic, and the nativistic movement takes on nationalistic (more in the sense of anti-Western) significance. Nationalism, instead of being a wholesome, positive, and creative movement, tends to become a morbid, negative, and reactionary or even escapist movement, while nativism, instead of being just a backward movement, tends to become a belligerent anti-foreignism.

. . . *Africa and Asia in Face of West: A Contrast*

The basic difference between the African and Asian situations seems to lie in the fact that in Africa there was no strong enough nation-state prior to European colonization, while in Asia it was the nation-states that the European powers colonialized. In Africa both ethnic solidarity and cultural integrity of the native population had been either nonexistent or broken up prior to the colonization by the West, while in Asia both had been maintained. For this reason, in Asian countries their peoples have seldom been alienated to the extent of becoming like "imported minorities" or foreigners in their own lands, though they were, like Africans, decidedly reduced to the status of "indigenous minorities."

This contrast between Asia and Africa in their respective reactions against the impact of the West may also be studied in terms of the types of civilizations that were prevailing in Asia and Africa at the time of the expansion of the West. By the same token, the differences among the colonial powers of the West—Great Britain, France, Belgium, Holland, Spain, Portugal, and Germany—both in terms of their own respective "national" culture, or ethos, and in terms of their colonial policies might have evoked different reactions on the part of colonialized peoples. Every case, however, can be generally conceived in terms of the majority-minority power relations. In thus generalizing the West without differentiating among the colonial powers, I include the U.S.A. in it, although she is not a colonial power in the usual sense of the term.

FOREIGN SETTLEMENTS AND CONCESSIONS

. . . *Case of China*

China, in my opinion, constitutes a unique case in the power relationships between the Afro-Asian countries and the West. China as a nation appears to have an incurable sense of self-confidence and self-importance, or what might be called a "majority psychology." Whether it is due to the vastness of the geographical area she covers, or to the antiquity of her culture, or to the type of civilization as represented by Confucianism, is immaterial to us at the moment. For many centuries the Chinese held that the whole of mankind was one great family in which he, the Chinese, was the elder brother and the rest were his younger brothers. The name of the country, Chung-Hua, indicates this better than anything else—"the central nation"! Furthermore, he was proud, and rightly so, of the culture which could be traced far back into antiquity—long before the Western civilization came into being.

To the Chinese, therefore, the overture made by the Western powers did not in any sense constitute a threat. China had always been ready to accept foreigners into her midst as long as the incoming foreigners were willing to "become Chinese" by assimilation. Those who would refuse to "become Chinese," or indigenized, might possibly be tolerated but never fully accepted. The great Jesuit missionary, Matteo Ricci, was fully accepted and highly regarded by the Imperial Court and the ruling aristocracy of seventeenth century China, but only at the expense of his relationship with the Papal office and other Roman Catholic missionary forces. Christianity was accepted because Matteo Ricci, by way of "accommodation," presented it as something intrinsically Chinese. But when the truth about Western Christianity was made manifest, Christianity was rejected completely. When later in the nineteenth century Protestant missionaries presented Christianity in its unabashedly Western formula, there was no interest shown in it by the Chinese. It was the Western missionaries, however, who made the farthest advance into the life of the Chinese. They were influential not as carriers of religious messages but rather as carriers of the Western technological civilization.

When the Western powers approached the Chinese government for the purpose of opening trade, China showed very little interest. In fact she had to be *forced* at the point of a gun to open herself for trade with the West. She had no interest in trade with the West because she was so firmly convinced that there was nothing of real value the West could offer to enrich her national culture or contribute to the welfare of her people. She therefore took a decidedly condescending attitude toward the "foreign devils," and when she could no longer resist their pressure, she decided to let them trade with her on her own terms. This, of course, was utterly unsatisfactory to the Western powers and they with their technical superiority forced their way into China, which of course evoked a violent reaction on the part of the Chinese. The Opium War and Boxer Rebellion were logical consequences of the strained and loaded relationships between them.

Finally, however, upon realizing how impossible it was to keep the Western powers out of her territory, China decided to let them have selected areas where they could have their own way, but not elsewhere. Thus foreign settlements and foreign concessions with extraterritoriality agreement were established in several key cities of the coastal area. They represented China's choice of the lesser evil of the two, the greater one being the complete overrunning of China by the West. To her it seemed much better to "give up" limited areas than to let the "foreign devils" go wild and infiltrate into all levels of national life, eventually causing her to lose her own "soul"—or cultural identity.

By the same token, China was perfectly willing to take in certain specific aspects of the Western civilization—those things of which she was sure she could make good use, but never Western civilization in its entirety. From her point of view no civilization could be better than her own and therefore it was utterly inconceivable that she allow her time-honored civilization to be replaced by such an upstart civilization as that of the West.

The attitude of the Chinese toward the encroaching Western civilization—whether via diplomacy, commerce or Christian missionary movement—was always that of condescension. But the intrinsic character of the technological civilization is such that adoption of any part of it inevitably leads to an all-pervading culture change, for, once allowed to step inside the country, it soon becomes an inner dynamic force that sets in motion a process of cultural change which will not stop short of a complete transformation of the old pattern of the national culture. China soon became aware that the impact made by the Western civilization was getting out of her control and could no longer be kept within the bounds of foreign settlements and concessions. In fact, before she knew it, China was being rapidly westernized from within herself. In other words, she was driven to realize that the only way to salvage her national autonomy and cultural integrity was to westernize herself rather than to resist the impact of the West. This, however, could not be done without a radical transformation of her traditional culture.

China's attitude toward the West has thus gone through several stages: first, there was *condescension*, then *resistance* (Boxer Rebellion), then *conformity* (in terms of blind imitation), and finally *revolt*. All the way through these different periods the attitude of China has been conditioned by a sense of hostility and opposition, and never by one of admiration and acceptance. China, between the time of the Boxer Rebellion and the Communist Revolution, at best tolerated the West within her national bounds and at worst was looking for an opportune moment to get rid of the West completely. With all sorts of superficial westernization in various aspects of her national life, the Chinese as a people did not really accept Western civilization. To think that they did is an illusion. It is in these lights that the meaning of the Communist Revolution of China must be assessed and that of her post-revolution nationalism. The revolution was basically not so much a movement *toward* the U.S.S.R. as a movement *away from* westernization, which in my opinion was inescapable.

COUNTRIES THAT CHOSE WESTERNIZATION

The two most conspicuous case histories in this category are Japan at the time of the Meiji Revolution and Turkey following the First World War. They both "found themselves confronted with a stark and inescapable choice between the whole-hearted westernization and outright extinction."[1] Both chose out-and-out westernization. For the purpose of illustrating my point, I refer to Japan, which I know much better than Turkey.

. . . *Case of Japan*

Since the turn of the nineteenth century the feudal life of Japan had been rapidly deteriorating, chiefly through the steady development of money economy. A large majority of the Samurai class (professional warriors and retainers of the feudal lords or Daimyo), of high prestige within a rigidly stratified society, who heretofore had been the lifeline of the defense and security of each feudal fief, were then turning into an economically unproductive class—finding themselves dependent for subsistence upon the once despised merchant class.

This critical situation reached its logical end with the collapse of the Tokugawa Shogunate, which coincided with, if it was not occasioned by, the Perry expedition (1853). Externally, that nation was faced with the challenge of an entirely new world situation characterized by the ever-

[1] Toynbee, A. J. *The World and the West,* p. 21. Columbus: Meridian Books, The World Publishing Company, 1958.

expanding power of the post-Industrial Revolution West. No longer was it possible for Japan to remain isolated from the rest of the world. The choice before her was either to stay unchanged and anticipate extinction or to adjust herself to this emerging new world and establish new relationships with the rest of the world, and more especially with the technologically advanced West. Internally, dispossessed Samurai played a unique role. As the elite of the old society, and having had the advantage of intellectual discipline, many of these ex-Sumurai took to the Western learning as their new vocation—their share in rebuilding their country or building a new Japan.

The Meiji Government was thus controlled by patriotic intellectuals of the former Samurai class—men who precisely because of their patriotism were extremely eager to westernize Japan, even though this would be accomplished at great cultural expense.

Japan's nationalism was thus not something that was aroused in reaction to the impact of the West, but rather it was motivated by her leaders' desire to westernize her national structure and economy. Japanese nationalism consequently has never taken the form of *nativism* in any sense. Her leaders expected to westernize the country sufficiently well for her to become respected in the new world. Confidence in this attitude prevailed until Japan had a rude awakening, notably at Versailles, that in spite of her conspicuous success in westernization, the Western powers deliberately refused to accept her as their peer. That was the moment when Japan within the international community of nations (then organized as the League of Nations) found herself an "alien minority" and since then her nationalism has taken on something of a nativistic character with a growing tendency of anti-Westernism, or xenophobia, with an increasing emphasis on the State Shinto and the "divine right" of the emperor. It is also against this background that one can begin to see the full implications of Japanese colonial imperialism in Asia, with its slogan "Asia for Asians."[2]

Prerequisite for Sound International Relations in Emerging World Community

Thus, perceiving these three major patterns of majority-minority tensions between the West and emerging nations in Asia and Africa suggests that a creative, wholesome, and genuine nationalism on the part of newly emerging nation-states is only possible when they are fully assured of their acceptance by the Western powers as independent, autonomous, and sovereign states on the basis of equality. By this it can be said that as long as the patterns of power relationships between Afro-Asian countries and the West remain unchanged, healthy development as nations can hardly be expected of countries in Asia and Africa, and to permit such a situation to continue is deliberately to perpetuate

[2] It must also be noted that following the defeat in the last war and the subsequent unconditional surrender to the Western powers, Japan has shown a remarkably friendly attitude toward the West, both under the military occupation of the allied forces and after regaining her independence. This was not exclusively due to the "enlightened occupation policy," as it has been frequently claimed, but rather due to the deep-seated desire on the part of Japan to westernize herself, the inception of which goes back to the Meiji Restoration. To Japan, since the Meiji period, the West has never been an evil to be resisted or an enemy to be kept at arm's length, but rather a model after which she should rebuild herself.

colonial imperialism on the part of many of the Western powers.

It is in the light of this that the significance of Bandung, 1955, and the emergence of something of an Afro-Asian bloc can be seen as a solidarity based on common protest or opposition against the West. It is against this background also that the seeming interest of Afro-Asian countries in the U.S.S.R. can best be assessed. Up to World War II there had been practically no history of majority-minority relationship between the U.S.S.R. and most of the Afro-Asian countries, whereas few of those countries had been completely free from the colonial domination of the West. This appears to be one of the reasons why some of these countries, especially the former colonies of the Western powers, tend to show interest in the U.S.S.R. At the same time this makes the position of the Western powers extremely awkward especially when they want to right their relationship with their former colonies.

One thing is eminently clear. There may be no greater folly for the West than to make anti-Communism the fundamental, let alone sole, principle to its relations to the Afro-Asian countries. To be insensitive to the racial undertones in its relations with the Afro-Asian peoples may very easily lead the West to take such a position.

The West, its power politics, commerce and industry, churches and missions all included, is now being judged by Afro-Asian peoples in terms of race relations. Knowing the kinds of power relations that have existed between the West and various Afro-Asian countries over the past couple of centuries, what are the Christians in the West to do, together with the Christians in the Afro-Asian countries, when these countries have at last gained political independence but still find themselves desperately dependent upon the West, economically and technically, while culturally they are as desperately asserting their own integrity and identity? How can the churches in the U.S.A. be effective missionary churches in a world in which, due to the heretofore prevailing patterns of race relations, the moral integrity of the West is so seriously questioned by the emerging new nations? These are the questions to which I shall address myself in the next chapter.

CHAPTER 6

Group Tensions in a Global Mass Society

One World Emergent

When I left Japan in 1937 to come to this country, the Pacific Ocean was a tremendous gulf that separated the Orient from the Americas. It took me nearly two weeks from Yokohama to San Francisco via a northern Pacific route—that is, without stopping at Honolulu. During my two years' study at General Theological Seminary in New York City (1937-39), I never used air mail to send my letters to my parents in Japan, for there was then no air mail service, international or domestic. Commercial passenger airplanes and air mail services became common only after World War II. The world then still consisted of "five continents and seven seas."

Today the Pacific Ocean is no longer a gulf separating the Orient and the Americas but more like a pond connecting the two. The fact that a war broke out between the U.S.A. and Japan in 1941 was one of the most convincing proofs that by then these two nations could no longer be kept apart from each other. They are geographically wider apart from each other than any other two nations in the world, and yet found themselves hitting at each other because the world had become too small for them to remain indifferent to each other. In such a world nations have to get along with one another or else they have to fight one another. There is no room for indifference to or disengagement with one another. This is the meaning of the term "one world" which we hear used so often nowadays.

When the late Wendell Wilkie used the term during his unsuccessful presidential campaign in 1940, it was quite a novel idea, and if my memory has not failed me, the public did not take to it very easily. But today it is of utmost importance that we recognize the simple truth that we are living in one world and that we think of, approach, and deal with the problem of race relations accordingly—that is, within the context of one world. In today's world no nation can be foreign to another and no racial or ethnic group can be totally alien to another, for all share in one and the same world, or an emerging world community. If we lose sight of this—or it should be said at this point, if we fail to see this—we shall not be looking at our problem in its proper perspective.

We experience the oneness of our world in many different ways. We do not have to travel all over the globe. If we only have our eyes open to see it, we literally cannot escape the one world anywhere. Travel, of course, helps to drive this home—the shortness of geographical distance from one continent to another, the common humanity that binds people of all sorts of nationalities and races, etc. In my personal observation there are two dimensions to the oneness of our world.

Interdependence of All Parts

In the first place all the nations are increasingly economically interdependent with one another and together are growing into one economic community. Industrial civilization has penetrated every part of the world. No country can now be self-sufficient either in terms of pre-industrial subsistence economy or in terms of the most advanced technological civilization. The dynamic nature of modern civilization does not permit any part of the world to remain unindustrialized. The more highly industrialized nations need less industrialized nations either as suppliers of raw material or as consumer markets.

All this has come about as an inevitable consequence of the colonial imperialism of the West in the post-Industrial Revolution period, and the modern foreign missionary movement of Western Protestantism has been an integral part of this expansion of the dynamic West. In this sense, and only in this sense, the whole world has been "westernized" as the late Professor Malinowski pointed out in his *Dynamics of Culture Change,* from his outlook as a cultural anthropologist. Professor Toynbee has been making the same point in many of his books and articles as an historian.

Anyone whose journey has taken him into remote sections of Africa and Asia cannot fail to be impressed by the extent to which the West with its technical civilization and industrial economy has penetrated. One French diplomat put it humorously: "After colonization, coca-cola-colonization." What was originally meant as a jibe at the "commercial imperialism" of the U.S. business enterprise may be taken as a symbol of the westernization of the contemporary world as a whole.

I am not for one moment suggesting that the entire world is now of one uniform culture as the result of westernization in the sense of the term used here. When Asian and African peoples finally adopted, or even yielded to, the dynamic industrial civilization with its distinctly Western marks, they indigenized it as well, except where the indigenous culture was completely wiped out by force. (I have seen segments of population in several countries formerly colonialized by Western powers who have been so thoroughly westernized that they were little less than foreigners in their own lands amongst their own compatriots.) After a generation or two of this two-way process of westernization of the indigenous culture and indigenization of the Western civilization there is now hardly what one might call "purely African" or "purely Asian" culture to be found in any country. To be sure, there are pockets of people in almost every country who have been left untouched by modern technical civilization, but the nation as a whole is no longer "purely" African or Asian insofar as the main stream of its culture is concerned, but increasingly "hybrid" —as hybrid as our so-called Western culture has always been—though with some distinguishable national characteristics remaining intact.

Dynamism of the Post-Industrial Revolution West

Parenthetically let me state how important it is for us to remember that the main agent of the unification of our contemporary world has been the civilization of the post-Industrial Revolution West. Parts of the world where it had not penetrated until World War I are now undergoing what is basically a cultural revolution, most notably the former Ottoman Empire and Latin America. The Ottoman Empire with its Islam-oriented culture successfully kept the West out of its boundaries for several centuries.

Today the countries where a highly developed civilization flourished in antiquity are farther apart from the West than Afro-Asian countries are, in terms of modern technical civilization. The Eastern Orthodox countries, including Greece, have suffered in this respect under the Turkish domination. Greece, for example, the cradle of Western civilization, had not been touched by the wave of dynamic expansion of Western Europe following the Industrial Revolution until she was liberated from Turkish rule.

On the other hand, Turkey, following World War I under the regime of Mustafa Kemal, pursued the drastic policy of out-and-out westernization. In the words of Professor Toynbee, "It was as if, in our Western world, the Renaissance, the Reformation, the secularist scientific mental revolution at the end of the 17th century, the French Revolution, and the Industrial Revolution had been telescoped into a single lifetime and been made compulsory by law."[1]

North and South Americas: Contrast

In this connection, the contrast between North America and Latin America is of tremendous interest to both the student of history and the student of social anthropology. The dynamism of North America undoubtedly stems from the fact that it was colonized by Anglo-Europeans of post-

[1] Toynbee, A. J. "The World and the West," *Documents on International Affairs,* pp. 27 f. Oxford: Oxford University Press, 1952.

Industrial Revolution vintage through successive waves of immigration. There is a sense in which Canada and the U.S.A. are an inevitable consequence of the Industrial Revolution in Great Britain and Western Europe.

South America, on the contrary, was colonized by Europeans from the Iberian Peninsula at the time when Portuguese and Spanish feudalism was at its height. Their colonists were of decidedly pre-industrial mentality and transplanted the pattern of medieval European feudalism to the New World, reducing the indigenous population to the status of serfdom. Herein is the cause for the stagnancy of Latin American countries, a state in which they have remained until recently. What is now happening throughout Latin America is the revolt of the masses, who have been exposed to the dynamic civilization of modern Western Europe as well as of North America, against their rulers of pre-industrial, feudalistic mentality. I have more than a sneaking suspicion that the U.S.A. is more directly instrumental than any other country for this cultural revolution that has been going on for the past decade or two in Latin American countries (cf. Frank Tannenbaum, *Ten Keys to Latin America*).

Similar Contrast Found in Africa

By the same token, in Africa there is conspicuous contrast between the territories under the rule of the British and West European countries on one hand, and those under Portuguese and Spanish rule on the other. Here, as in the Americas, the dynamics of the emerging one world have been obliterating the geo-political boundary lines between one country and another so that even in Angola and Mozambique the pre-modern pattern of colonial rule is doomed soon to be over.

In the same vein I might suggest that the basic trouble with the Republic of South Africa lies in the fact that it was first colonized by a group of pre-industrial Dutch farmers, intensely religious, to establish a commonwealth based on what they believed was the biblical blueprint, and later by the post-Industrial Revolution Britons. To the Afrikaners, the descendants of the early Dutch colonists, South Africa alone is their homeland, whereas to the British South Africans, Britain is their homeland and South Africa is only a colony of Britain. This basic difference of outlook cannot but create conflict between them, and the battle has been fought in terms of their pronounced policies on race relations. (I say pronounced policies, not practices, advisedly.) In terms of pre-industrial, agricultural civilization in which landed gentry and serfdom constituted two distinct castes, the Afrikaner farmers' treatment of the African farm hands is neither unchristian nor inhuman. In fact, most of them are devout Christians and extremely considerate towards their African farm hands. The only trouble is that they are still living in sixteenth and seventeenth century Europe, while their African farm hands are living in the twenty-first century (when they hope they will have been completely freed from the yoke of white domination).

Man's Outlook Still Pre-Industrial Revolution

One world is thus to a great extent an accomplished reality in the realm of economics and technology wherein we all are now living. One world is still at an embryonic stage in the realm of man's mentality or in terms of the growth of a worldwide human community. This is precisely our problem. We are not contemporary with our age. Living in the last half of the twentieth century, benefiting from the most highly developed technology in every sphere of our life, our mentality still seems to be several centuries behind time especially when it comes to the matter of human relations! "Our" nation, "our" culture, "our" race, and often enough "our" tribe seem to be strong enough controlling assumptions as we face "other" people though all are now living in one and the same economic orbit throughout the world. (When I mention tribes, I want my readers not to forget the tensions between the Irish and English in Britain, which has even been carried over to the U.S. scene, or Swedes and Norwegians in Minnesota, for that matter, as well as the inter-tribal conflicts in Africa or among American Indians in this country.)

This last point leads us to consider the second dimension of the oneness of our world, which is the increasingly international character of the local communities. There is a sense in which the world as a whole is shrinking into a neighborhood and simultaneously every neighborhood is growing into a world community. At least the characteristics which are making our world into one world are being embodied in every local community. In one of his articles Professor Paul Tillich said that ours is an age in which the world situation constantly jumps into the local situation, or something to this effect.[2]

[2] It was in an issue of the *Anglican Theological Review* which I happened to be reading on the bus leaving Tule Lake Relocation Center in which I had been confined for about one year (1942-43). Reading under these peculiar circumstances what Professor Tillich said struck me so strongly that to this day I cannot help being moved by it.

Many an overseas journey I have had since then has thoroughly convinced me how right Professor Tillich's statement is. A few years ago I looked up a Cambridge student of anthropology near Lake Victoria in the Nyanza Province of Kenya, where he was doing an original research among African people relatively untouched by white people. He was living in a tent which he pitched on a mission school ground. When I arrived there totally unannounced he was not in. His cook who spoke hardly any English led me further into the bush and, keeping me waiting there, he went on to fetch my man, who, upon hearing that there was a Japanese man looking for him, wondered whether his knowledge of the tribal language was woefully inadequate or his cook had gone out of his mind! Skeptically he came out and when he saw me standing there he had to doubt his own eyes! Amazingly though, the African children who instantly congregated on the spot did not seem to think it such an extraordinary event. Subsequently in several places in Africa I ran into African men who had fought the Japanese forces in Burma and Malaya. Japanese people are no longer entirely unknown to the African people even in the most remote part of the continent.

Case of Britain

In 1960-61 there were a series of race riots in England, of which Notting Hill, London, received the widest publicity, though it was by no means the only or the most serious incident that occurred. The Act of Parliament (the Commonwealth Immigrant Act) in the attempt to control the influx of immigrants from the commonwealth nations, especially the West Indies, India, and Pakistan, was widely interpreted as discriminatory against the colored immigrants because the restrictions did not apply to Irish immigrants. At any rate this act of Parliament forced the British people, especially the English, to re-examine their outlook on the race problem.

Unlike the U.S.A. the British Isles until recently had few people of colored races. It can be said that the British "solved" the race problem outside of the British Isles, namely in their colonies, where the problem took an entirely different form from what it would have been at home. But now the colored people from the former colonies are coming into the British Isles, not as aliens but as members of the British Commonwealth, and the problem has taken on an entirely new meaning.

In Birmingham—during my six-week visit to Britain early in 1962—I was a guest of the Methodist International House one evening. After supper I sat in the lounge with a group of students for an informal discussion. Among them were two Chinese students and I was curious to know whether they were from the mainland China, Hong Kong, or Taiwan, but one of them told me he was from Sarawak and the other from Trinidad. Then I turned to three Indian students, none of whom, as it turned out, was from India: one from Ceylon, one from Tanganyika, and one from Durban, South Africa. There were two Englishmen, I thought, in the group, but one turned out to be an Australian and the other a Northern Rhodesian! I commented on this as an interesting sign of our time and they said: "You yourself are not doing too badly either—born in Taiwan, reared in Japan, a naturalized U.S. citizen, living in Switzerland, visiting England, and talking about Africa!" Thereupon the Rev.

J. J. Whitfield, my host in Birmingham, who incidentally seems to have done more to improve race relations in that city than any other single individual in his quiet but untiring manner, pulled a notebook out of his pocket and read a list of people who attended one of his friends when taken to a Birmingham hospital following an automobile accident: The ambulance driver was a West Indian, the attending nurse a Chinese, the doctor at the receiving room of the hospital a Pakistani, one of the orderlies who pushed him into the ward an African. This, said J. J., is Birmingham today. It is a hard place for anyone who has race prejudice to live in!

Empire Comes Home

What has been happening to Britain since World War II is what has been happening all over the world, only a little more intensely there than elsewhere. Great Britain has been an empire builder, and in this enterprise, employers, adventurers, statesmen, political philosophers, industrialists, military men, a host of civil servants, and last but not least, successions of Christian missionaries, have collaborated. British colonial imperialism was, at least partially, motivated by a profound sense of mission—mission to civilize the world after her own pattern, as is seen in the most straightforward motto of David Livingstone: "Commerce and Christianity" to liberate the African people from the evil of the slave trade.

In other areas the same motto was applied to liberate the indigenous population from slavery to various forms of superstitions and primitive ways of life. Britain has to a large measure been successful insofar as the building of an empire for herself is concerned, though the question which may still remain unanswered is whether this has achieved the noble ideal behind her imperialism, namely the liberation of indigenous peoples from all forms of the practice of slavery.

And now suddenly—or it only seems to be sudden—"the empire is coming home," as my friend the Rev. Marcus James, a Jamaican, then the incumbent of St. Peter's Parish, Stepney, London, has so aptly put it. Indeed the West Indian people regard England as their "mother country"—they have been British all these years, and England is where the British way of life originates.

More objectively speaking, not only the West Indians, but also Indians and Pakistanis, and increasingly Africans, have been migrating into Britain in recent years because these far-flung parts of the Commonwealth have become just as much economic hinterlands of metropolitan England as Ireland has traditionally been. This is the same economic principle that characterizes the relationships between the urban-industrial cities and the surrounding rural areas within any nation today. As the phenomenon of rural exodus is inevitable, so is the migration into metropolitan Britain from all parts of her Commonwealth. To try to curb it, let alone stop it, is not to come to terms with the reality of the one world in which every local community is bound to take on an international character both in its population makeup and its culture. The diversities of people from every corner of the earth due to their environment and cultural heritage are now coexisting. The fact is that racial, cultural, and religious pluralism will soon prevail everywhere in the world.

Race Relations in World Perspective

It is in the light of this prospect that we ought to think of the problem of race relations. (This also forces us to rethink the *mission* of Christian "missions," of which more will be said later.) To be preoccupied with "how to prevent my children from marrying outside of my race," or "how to save the 'white civilization' in its pure and uncontaminated state," etc., is to continue to live in the pre-industrial, medieval age, and is thoroughly unchristian in that it does not recognize the acts of God in history, as if God had stopped acting with, say, the Protestant Reformation! God has acted in history through the Industrial Revolution, American Revolution, French Revolution, and even the Russian Revolution.

God is acting in the contemporary Afro-Asian and Latin American revolutions which are by nature more cultural than political, and in which the Christian churches in the West have been more than instrumental, however inadvertently or unwittingly, for it has been the Christian gospel more than any other single factor that has aroused in the Afro-Asian and Latin American peoples the profound sense of their own human dignity. Having thus participated in the divine act in history, are we now to turn around and say, "Oh, we did not mean to go that far"? To discriminate against people solely on the basis of race, color or ethnic origin in this day and age is a historical anachronism before it is immoral. Historical anachronism is just as serious a form of apostasy as immorality for it is just as much a disobedience to God who has revealed himself through his acts in history.

One World Through Interpenetration

The two dimensions of the oneness of our world as we have seen may be stated in still another way. From the standpoint of the West, Asia and Africa have at first been appended to it through its colonial imperialism. Various parts of Africa and Asia became significant to the West only insofar as they served the needs of the West. What Professor Owen Lattimore said in 1945 about Asia can now be said about Africa and Latin America: "Asia was for several centuries an area in which political history and the economic fate of hundreds of millions of people were determined by things that happened somewhere outside of Asia.

"We have now crossed over into a period in which things happening in Asia, opinions formed in Asia, and decisions made in Asia, will largely determine the course of events elsewhere in the world."[3] In other words it was not merely the civilization of the West that penetrated the rest of the world, nor were Asia, Africa, and Latin America annexed to the West, but they have been incorporated into the life of the West and the West itself has become incorporated into their life. This mutual, two-way involvement between the West and the rest of the world is what makes one global community of our world.

What I discussed in the two previous chapters, namely race relations in terms of power relations between dominant and subordinate, or majority and minority groups within one nation, and similar tensions with strong racial

[3] Lattimore, Owen. *Solution in Asia,* p. 1. London: The Cresset Press, 1945.

undertones between the West and the now emerging nations, must be seen within the context of the emerging one world community. It seems to me that modern man, irrespective of his race, color, or nationality, senses almost instinctively that the traditional pattern of nation-state is now rapidly becoming obsolete; in fact he sees that no human group can remain a closed group in the kind of global community that is dawning upon the world, and is suffering from an acute sense of insecurity about his place and uncertainty concerning his future in this new world.

Technology is color-blind. Man's worth in "secular" terms is no longer dependent on his family background, ancestry, racial and ethnic stock, or even nationality, but on his technical skills, scientific knowledge, and accompanying creativity. This, however, is a terrible threat to many people, especially to those who have long been used to enjoying power and prestige, not on the basis of their skills or achievements but simply because they happened to belong to the dominant race in their society. It is mostly such people who are fighting the last-ditch fight against the principle of open and equal opportunity for all people regardless of their race, color, ethnic origin, or religion.

Racial Equality: An Inevitability in Industrial Civilization

In the Copperbelt of Northern Rhodesia the principal of one of the European high schools shared with me his grave concern as an educator. Most of his students were not interested in going to universities or even receiving technical training in one profession or another, nor were the majority of their parents, for that matter. The reason was that with their white skin they could get well-paid jobs in the mining industry without any special skills, and immediately boss over African workers who do all the hard work. With only seven or eight years of schooling, they would live ten times as well as they could in Britain or anywhere in the West—not only the undeservedly fat salary, but also the nice housing attached to the job, a couple of servants, an automobile, and membership in exclusive clubs.

To such people the African advancement program initiated by the mining industry several years ago has been a real threat and the prospect of "black government" is too awful to think about. When I was there in 1961, however, even the poltically conservative English-language newspaper, *The Northern News,* editorialized: "No Place for Unskilled Europeans," and urged the parents of school-going children to encourage their children to take schooling more seriously.

At the same time, the African nationalists were demanding that the government provide equal educational opportunities for African and European children, for they became fully aware that in the emerging new society man without productive skills would be completely out of luck and so far they had been denied the right to receive education simply because they were Africans. Racial consciousness was thus accentuated on both sides because the dynamics of the technological civilization were relentlessly obliterating the functional significance of racial distinction!

A similar situation is prevailing all over the world whereever a particular racial group has traditionally occupied the dominant position over others. Racial tensions cannot possibly be resolved in such a situation without the people involved first coming to grips with the reality of the one world community. "Harmony between persons of different racial origins does not depend upon their being properly informed about the latest findings of modern anthropology!"[4]

Mission of the Church

The mission of the church in the contemporary world cannot avoid dealing with the racial issues, but it cannot be fulfilled by directly attacking the racial problems as such, much less by merely multiplying missionary enterprises for racial or ethnic groups or by intensifying the exhortations to members of the dominant groups to be more tolerant and considerate toward members of the subordinate groups. All these ought to be renounced once and for all as a sacrilege insofar as they are conceived as methods of resolving racial problems, for they are paternalistic, irrelevant, and anachronistic! The church's mission is one among all people everywhere and all the time—that is, to proclaim to them what God is doing now in their midst, with them and upon them as well as for them. To put it differently, it is to bring people up to date with the act of God in history, help them to be more contemporaneous with the reality of God's creation at the present moment.

So many of us, devout Christians though we may be, when preoccupied with the race problem, would not go much beyond the Book of Genesis (and often not more than Chapter IX at that!) in seeking to find what God's will or design is on matters pertaining to races of mankind. Or, some of us, taking pride in being something of Protestant

[4] Little, Kenneth. "Race and Society," in *The Race Question in Modern Science,* p. 166. Paris: UNESCO, 1956.

iconoclasts in regard to many matters of doctrine, liturgy, holy orders, church polity, etc., suddenly become rigid traditionalists when confronted by the question whether or not to change the old pattern of race relations within the institutional structure of our own churches and in our own towns or cities, saying, "Let us not be too hasty." Both of these attitudes and a thousand and one variations of them, with which we all are quite familiar, have one thing in common—that is, to assume that God stopped working at a certain point in history. As I said earlier we may not have or condone such a manifestly wrong thing as a "restrictive covenant" within the church—at least openly—but in fact we do infinitely worse by arbitrarily *restricting* God's action up to a certain point in history. If this is not a sacrilege or an apostasy I do not know what is.

A Christian Ethic of Learning

What Professor Kenneth Boulding once said in dealing with another problem as knotty as race—economic issues and their ethical implications—I believe, is applicable to our present concern. "Two elements in the Biblical ethic seem peculiarly relevant for today's world: the ethic of repentance and the ethic of meekness. Both of these can be gathered under the single heading of the ethic of learning: 'Teach me thy way O Lord.' By repentance we become willing to unlearn. . . . By meekness we become willing to learn. The meek inherit the earth because they are adaptable and learn fast. . . ."[5] All of us who have grown up in

[5] Boulding, Kenneth, "The Ethical Perspective," *The Fourth National Study Conference on the Church and Economic Life,* Pittsburgh, Nov. 8-11, 1962.

a world divided into many parts and segments, by race, color, ethnic origin, nationality, and many other things, must now *unlearn* as quickly as possible the old and familiar ways and learn as fast as possible what the emerging one world community demands of us, more specifically in the areas of inter-group and inter-personal relationships. This is an absolute prerequisite for us in order to be contemporaneous with our age—that is, to keep up with what God has been doing in and through the revolutionary changes throughout the world creating a one world community out of many nations and tongues. It is the doing of the same God who "made from one every nation of men to live on all the face of the earth, having determined allotted periods and the boundaries of their habitation." To proclaim this wonderful news and to bring all its implications home to men and women of this generation, Christians and non-Christians alike, is the most important mission God has commissioned his church to carry out at this juncture of history—nothing more nor less.

CHAPTER 7

Tragedy of Man Estranged from God

From the last chapter we can see that we are living in a desperately paradoxical situation today. The very forces working to create a one world community are also pitting people of many different ethnic and cultural backgrounds against one another within the context of one community everywhere in the world. The dynamics of modern society somehow accentuate racial, ethnic, and national consciousness for everyone. When the objective situation makes it imperative that men get over the group differences which have in the past divided them, group consciousness seems to become more acute than ever. This paradox constitutes the peculiar context in which the race relations problem of this generation must be seen. There is a sense in which this paradox points to the basic characteristics of modern man's environment, both external and internal, apart from which neither he nor his problems can be fully understood.

Group Consciousness Intensified in Mass Society

Human society is always a group of groups and not made up of unattached individuals. As Professor Edgar T. Thompson has put it, "A society is a group within which smaller groups are in a continuous state of interaction."[1] Inter-group tensions or power relations between groups are therefore a normal state of affairs in a living human society. Such being the case, we cannot expect all sorts of groups, large and small, completely to disappear even when the now emerging world community reaches its full maturity. The question is what place the ethnically oriented or racially based groups occupy or should occupy among all other groups in the kind of society in which we are now living—a growing world community.

First let us see how group consciousness based on racial or ethnic distinction is being intensified in many parts of the world and in a number of different ways. As an illustration, we may turn our attention to Nigeria on the eve of her independence (achieved in October, 1960). Here we find most of the issues with which we are concerned in acute form.

Nigeria is made up of three provinces, Western, Eastern, and Northern. Lagos, the seat of the Federal Government, was a British Crown Colony and the three provinces were together a British protectorate. The population has been estimated very roughly between 30 and 35 million with an infinitesimal proportion of Europeans (in the neighborhood of five thousand).

I spent exactly one month in Nigeria, a few months prior to her independence, traveling through all three provinces. At that time nothing was more important to Nigeria than national unity—which in practical terms meant nothing less

[1] Thompson, E. T. and Hughes, E. C. (eds.) "Society as a Group of Groups," in *Race: Individual and Collective Behavior*, p. 315. Glencoe: Free Press, 1958.

than integration of the three provinces. (To be precise, I must mention that a small part of the Cameroons, a British trusteeship territory, was then a part of Nigeria, too, but for our present purpose it is not so important to include it.) Paradoxically, however, there was a strongly decisive force at work toward *regionalism*—that is, to insist on the autonomy of provincial governments, each of which was dominated by a specific ethnic group: North by Hausa, East by Ibo, and West by Yoruba. The situation was further complicated by religious factors. In both the Western and Eastern provinces, Christian missions had done a very effective job. Here, a high proportion of the indigenous population (approximately 60 per cent) were Christians—perhaps higher than almost any other African country. But in the Northern Province, Muslim chiefs had ruled for a long period under the British colonial policy of "indirect rule." The British Government, in deference to the Muslim chiefs, had officially discouraged the Christian missions from going into the Northern Province.

As we have seen in the preceding chapter, technological civilization had been penetrating every part of Africa, causing an increasing number of people to become footloose and mobile on one hand, and on the other, bringing geographically separated areas into more and more economic interdependence. Northern Nigeria, for example, found itself in a peculiar situation in that its civil service posts were largely filled by Eastern and Western Nigerians and expatriates. So were a majority of skilled positions in private industries and self-employed traders all over the province. This meant that while party politics were dominated by Muslims the business of the government was run by Christians and economic and industrial development was pretty much in the hands of people from other provinces. At the time of my visit to Northern Nigeria everybody was talking about the "northernization" policy of its government. By this they meant that any public position that could be filled by a Northerner must not be held by an outsider. To those posts for which they could find no qualified Northerner, they would appoint outsiders until qualified Northerners became available, and in this case they would prefer expatriates, i.e., Africans from other countries or even Europeans, to Nigerians from the eastern or western region.

This policy was commonly interpreted by the expatriate missionaries (as well as resident Western and Eastern Nigerians) as the first step of the Northern government in establishing a Muslim state and, as such, one form of persecuting Christians. They pointed out to me that Christian missions were welcome to stay in Northern Nigeria if they would run schools to educate Northerners' children. Schools at every level were at a premium. Government-subsidized schools were required by law to have 75 per cent or more Northerners, and proselytism in schools was strictly prohibited. Such legal restriction was interpreted by Christian missions as an unquestionable indication of the anti-Christian policy of the Northern government. The fact of the matter, however, was that Christians among the Northerners were just as vehemently pro-northernization as Muslims—I learned this from talking with both sides. It was *indigenization* of everything that was of utmost importance in their minds, not *Islamization!*

Here, then, was a collective attempt of the Northerners to

assert their ethnic identity and regional integrity. And in this attempt there was no difference between Christians and Muslims. I am afraid that neither expatriate missionaries working in Northern Nigeria nor Nigerian Christians in the Eastern and Western Provinces truly understood this or appreciated its true significance. For all I heard from them was that Christians *qua* Christians were in for a period of persecution and ostracism.

Skill in Industrial Society

It is, however, not the whole truth. Nearer the truth is to recognize that in industrial economy and technological civilization people find their places in society where their skills are wanted—that is, where they prove most useful or where they can make the most of what they have, be it a technical skill, a piece of machinery, a tool, capital, or an artistic talent. I was, for example, astounded by the number of Syro-Lebanese traders in Sierra Leone and Liberia in 1957. Then there was no class of entrepreneurs among the citizens of Liberia (the oldest independent nation in Africa south of the Sahara except Ethiopia). Liberian society consisted of only a small number of elite and a predominant majority of mass. The elite were plantation-owners and politicians. The masses were tribesmen turned daily-paid workers on the plantations or a rapidly growing urban proletariat. The gap between them created by the introduction of money economy into that part of West Africa was filled by the most enterprising traders from Lebanon, Syria and the neighboring Arab countries.

In Sierra Leone an appreciable number of Arab traders have been permanently settled and their businesses have been indigenized, although old connections with the Arab world are being maintained to the advantage of both the developing Sierra Leone and themselves. In Liberia, which is intended to be a 100 per cent Negro republic, naturalization of people who are not Negro is prohibited by the national constitution. Syro-Lebanese traders are not allowed to hold title to any real property. This means, one may assume, that a goodly portion of their profit made in Liberia is going out of the country. Still they are there because they can make money and the Liberian economy needs them and what they bring in with them. And a remarkable thing is that both in Sierra Leone and Liberia one notices hardly any friction between the indigenous Africans and Syro-Lebanese traders. Because their sole interest in Liberia is economic, they seem so far to have enjoyed something more than a peaceful co-existence.

I wonder why there should be such a difference between the ethnic tensions in Northern Nigeria and the interracial harmony in Sierra Leone and Liberia. I wonder also how long the peaceful relationships between Africans and Syro-Lebanese will last in these latter countries. It will be idle for us to speculate on these questions in the abstract. Let me cite a couple more situations like these from other parts of the world.

In December, 1960, I accidentally witnessed a near race-riot in the City of Nairobi, Kenya. Those who have read about the Mau Mau crisis of Kenya (1952) would not be surprised by the news of a race riot in Nairobi but may well be surprised to hear that it was not a riot of Africans against Europeans but against Indians. I had no idea how fierce the tensions had been between the Africans and Indians in

Kenya and in East Africa in general. Against the Indians all the African tribes seem to be solidly united! In one of the small group meetings I attended during my short stay in Kenya, I heard one of the Christian ministers of Kikuyu background saying to the European and Indian Christians present: "The Europeans have done a lot of good for us as well as dominated and humiliated us. They brought Christianity and technology. They opened up our country, modernized it, educated us, and trained us toward independence. If, therefore, they repent now for the wrongs they have done in the past, we are more than glad to have them stay with us after we have gained independence. As for the Indians, it is an entirely different matter. They have not done one blessed good for us. They have stood between the Europeans and the Africans, preventing us from advancing faster. They can expect no place in an independent Kenya." This indeed was an extremely strong statement and a disturbing one, too, coming from a Christian minister. I personally was glad that he said it openly and in such a matter-of-fact tone of voice, for this undoubtedly was what the rank and file of Africans were thinking about the Indians in their midst.

It was this sentiment long pent up in them that exploded when an automobile driven by an Indian man hit an African pedestrian and tried to run away. Within a minute the whole African location was "up in arms," and all over the area every car driven by an Indian was being attacked! Knowing nothing about what was going on, I was with an English lady in her Volkswagen, driving a Kikuyu couple to their home in the location and literally "walked into" the scene of the riot. Our Kikuyu companion sizing up the situation said, "Betty, you are safe. They are not after Europeans. Dai, you had better hide, they are after Indians." Unable to make myself hidden inside the small Volkswagen, I exposed myself in full, whereupon my Kikuyu friend said: "Now you are all right. They have seen that you are a Japanese!" In those few moments I saw on the faces of African people there assembled a curious mixture of utterly unsophisticated goodness and irrepressible hatred—the two qualties which normally cannot go together at all!

That night I was more saddened than frightened by what this incident implied. For one thing I realized that Nairobi was then sitting on a keg of dynamite with triangular racial tensions about which apparently no measure was being taken either by the government, the churches, or any civic organizations. But, why should the Africans have such an intense hatred against the Indians? The question haunted me all night long. In the barest outline the answer may be sketched as follows:

Kenya was colonized by Englishmen and developed as a country of large-scale commercial agriculture, including tobacco and coffee plantations and cattle ranches. Colonists became the landed gentry and Africans their serfs. At the time of the construction of the Uganda Railway Indians were brought over as cheap labor because either Africans were unwilling to do such hard labor or they were regarded as unfit for it. When the construction of the railway was finished most of the Indians declined to accept repatriation, stayed on in East Africa and became petty traders, "filling a gap in the economic structure of the country by opening dukas in every embryonic township and trading cheap blankets and trinkets to the natives, but draining money steadily out of the country to India."[2]

As this statement by a world-renowned author of many books on East Africa indicates, Indians as traders have played a decisively important role in modernizing East Africa in the inter-war period and have formed an indispensable middle class between the English colonists and the increasingly dispossessed African masses. Thus the economic stratification of Kenya society coincided with racial distinction and "class war" was *ipso facto* racial conflict. As time elapsed and more and more Africans received education, became Christians, and adopted the Englishman's way, the distance between the colonists and Africans became less and less than either between the colonists and the Indians or between the Indians and the Africans, at least in terms of culture and religion. Indians, with the exception of a few Goanese who are Roman Catholics, have persistently remained unconverted to Christianity—most of them seem to be Sikhs—and have retained Indian customs unaltered. As is often the case with emigrant groups of any nationality, Indians in East Africa are likely to be more Indian than Indians at home. In recent years, therefore, there has been much more in common between the Englishmen and the Africans in East Africa than either between the Indians and the Africans or between Englishmen and the Indians. For both the English colonists and the Africans Kenya is home, while for the Indians it is not; India still is.

In spite of all this there has been no change in the Afri-

[2] Huxley, Elspeth. *White Man's Country,* Vol. I, p. 64. London: Macmillan Company, 1935.

cans' social status and they have been justifiably indignant about it. They have interpreted it to mean several things: (1) that the Englishmen, out of deep-seated racial prejudice against the Africans, are using the Indians as a buffer to stop African advancement; or (2) that the Indians are capitalizing on this situation and exploiting the Africans. The Africans thus assume that had it not been for these Indians, they could have improved their own position much more easily. Not only in Kenya but all over East Africa and British Central Africa much of the labor-management conflict is *de facto* racial strife, not exclusively between the white and the African, but frequently with the Indians thrown in between them.

Mobility of Man in Open Society

No society is completely static and closed, or completely dynamic and open. Insofar as a society continues to exist from one generation to the next there are in it elements which remain more or less unchanged or change extremely slowly. These elements give stability to the society and sometimes create an impression that that society is static and unchanging.

Insofar as any society cannot exist in isolation from the rest of the world, it is both dynamic and open. Relatively speaking, the pre-industrial and particularly feudalistic society was more static and closed, whereas industrial society is more dynamic and open. In the former, class distinction was rigid and hereditary; vertical mobility from one class to another was practically nonexistent. In the latter, class distinction has little meaning and vertical mobility between classes is one of the keys that safeguard the dynamic nature of the society as a whole. In the one, the social class into which a man was born determines his post in the society; in the other, a man's initiative, ability, and skill (acquired or developed) can open up opportunities, determine his place in the society, and even change his social status.

If the three racial communities were stratified by color in the pre-industrial society, the problem might not have been too serious, as, for example, in the southern United States during the plantation economy (I am not condoning slavery by saying this), or in Sierra Leone and Liberia, until relatively recently. But in the industrial society of today, it is bound to create serious problems unless the right to move vertically as well as horizontally is assured for every person regardless of his race, color, or ethnic origin.

In an industrial society which by its very nature is international in character and pluralistic in composition (as has been discussed in the last chapter), a group which by race or color is barred from the arena of competition is bound to become acutely race conscious. The cases of Northern Nigeria and Kenya, each in its own way, illustrate this point.

From the several situations described above, we may be able to say that it is not so much race *per se* that causes trouble as man's group consciousness, or the roles various kinds of human groups seem to play in an increasingly dynamic and open society—a society which by its very nature insists on evaluating man solely on his capacity to produce. The one world community of which much has been said on the preceding pages is going to be a "mass society" in the best sense of the term, in which nothing counts as much as one's ability to contribute to the well-being of the society.

In-Group and Out-Group in Mass Society

In such a society, there can be no "in-group" fixed on a permanent basis, nor can one entirely or forever remain alien (foreigner or outsider) to another. That is, however, not to say that all groups less than the world community will be completely obliterated. On the contrary, groups will remain. They may even tend to solidify themselves. At least man may become more acutely conscious of the group with which either he is identified by the society at large, or with which he in his own mind identifies himself.

What really matters is the change that comes over the pattern of interaction between groups. In a less dynamic community, artistocrat and commoner, though functionally dependent upon each other, do not engage in dialogue with each other. In an industrial community, management and labor are not only dependent on each other to keep industry going but are constantly engaged in collective bargaining, which is an institutionalized process of two-way dialogue.

In a pre-industrial society, for example, medieval feudalism, social groups and sub-groups were hereditary and closed communities, permanently dividing the populace into insiders and outsiders. In such a society, to marry outside one's own group or class was regarded as an inexcusable offense to one's in-group; all sorts of *taboos* were invented to prevent this from happening. In a mass society, such as ours is turning out to be, none of the groups are entirely hereditary or closed, although each of them does maintain its own identity and integrity. Therefore, none of them permanently divides people into insiders and outsiders. This means, among other things, there is in principle no such thing as marrying in one's group or outside it. Marriage between individuals belonging to different groups is happening all the time. To employ any device to prevent this is to try to turn the clock back for several centuries into the ages before the Industrial Revolution. The question of interracial marriage, too, must be dealt with in this perspective.

Marriage, Inter-Group and Intra-Group

Intra-group marriage was a political device by which to perpetuate the social groups in a society in which the hereditary group determines the position of man and his worth. In the contemporary society, inter-group rather than intra-group marriages have become more frequent, simply because the society as a whole has become more dynamic and open by nature and its population increasingly mobile. More people meet across their group boundaries, in every imaginable way—social class, nationality, profession, race. This is only natural or is in keeping with the trend of the growth and development of the one world community. In saying all these things, however, I am not for one moment advocating interracial marriage as a means to further a cause of integration of different racial groups with one another. Marriage must never be used as a means for something else. Interracial marriage takes place when it does between individuals who have transcended their racial difference. It should not be conceived of as a means to achieve a racially integrated society.

The plight of children born to parents who are married across racial lines simply indicates how anachronistic much of our society is. Economically and industrially though they are living in the latter half of the twentieth century, a great proportion of modern men are still holding on to a pre-modern, feudalistic concept of human relations. Such people as the *Colored* in South Africa, the *Euro-Africans* in British Central Africa, the *Eurasians* in Asia, the *Burghers* in Ceylon, or those of mixed racial parentage in the U.S.A.—they belong neither to one racial community nor to another. Rejection comes from one group for one reason, from the other for another. That is their fate in present society, and it will continue to be as long as the society stays under the spell of the old in-group and out-group way of thinking. If we are to be consistent at all they should belong fully to both groups.

There is absolutely no point in condemning interracial marriage, for there is nothing wrong whatsoever with it theologically, morally, or biologically. *Theologically*—man was created, male and female, after God's own image; race, color, and ethnic background having nothing to do with his being what he is. *Morally*, there is nothing more required of a mature man and a mature woman than to love and respect each other and in freedom to enter into the total relationship of giving and receiving by mutual agreement. *Biologically*, "men belong to one mating circle, and share in a common pool of genes."[3] In terms of civil and human rights, in an avowedly democratic society such as ours, mature men and women have every right to marry those they choose.

Having said all that I have said on the subject of inter-

[3] Dunn, L. C. "Race and Biology," in *The Race Question in Modern Science*, p. 276. Paris: UNESCO, 1956.

racial marriage, I must hasten to add a word—not to make any new point but to reiterate what has already been stated at least by implication—namely, marriage is between two persons and not between two groups, racial or otherwise; the relationship which is the result of marriage is a personal one, independent of any kind of group relationship; and a man can marry only one woman at one time. It is a private affair.

As a matter of fact, not to have any sort of *a priori* restriction upon the circle from whom one may choose one's life-time mate makes the decision-making process infinitely more difficult than to have the circle narrowed down by somebody else! With all the vehement speeches we make on freedom—glorifying it, demanding it for us and others—we are in fact profoundly afraid of it because it demands so much of us. "Unlimited liberty is a torment and ruination to man," but "without freedom there is no man. . . ." and "the way of freedom is the way of suffering, and man must follow it to the end."[4] As Dr. Erich Fromm has shown to us through many of his writings, most of us cannot bear the burden of freedom and try everything we can to "escape from freedom." Parents who categorically eliminate men of one group or another, racial or otherwise, as potential husbands of their daughters, are not only denying their daughters the freedom to choose their own mates, which is one of their human and civil rights, but also are manifesting their own anxiety to be free. Only when man is a new creation in Christ, in whom there is neither Jew nor Greek, neither bond nor free, is he truly free. For only in his com-

[4] Berdyaev, Nicholas. *Dostoevsky,* Ch. 2.

plete surrender to Christ man finds "two freedoms: freedom to choose the truth and freedom in the truth."[5]

Modern Man in Search of His Identity

It is essentially because of his fear of being totally free in a completely open, mass society that modern man is so desperately trying to identify himself with one in-group or another. For centuries, this has been what gave man his sense of belongingness, of having his roots down, and of knowing objectively who he is. "We" is a qualitative content of the "I."[6]

Man who is not in Christ is incapable of identifying himself with the whole of mankind and therefore is bound to identify himself with a lesser group, or series of such groups, so that he may be able to say "we," but in so doing he is setting up, in his own mind, "they," the outsiders, over against "we," the insiders. "We" is reduced to "I and my kind." It is this *restrictive* process of the circle with which modern man can comfortably identify himself that traps him into the new form of racism today, in spite of all the findings of modern biological and anthropological sciences, all the biblical exegesis and theological expositions on the teachings of Jesus and of his church.

Man estranged from God, the ground of his being, loses his self-identity. He no longer knows who and what he truly is. Consequently he cannot relate himself to his fellow man simply as a man; he has to have the assurance that this man belongs to his group. Modern mass society is,

[5] Berdyaev, *op. cit.*, Ch. 3.

[6] Berdyaev, *Slavery and Freedom*, tr. by R. M. French, p. 103. New York: Charles Scribner's Sons, 1944.

therefore, an awful place to live in for man whose life is not rooted in "the blessed company of all faithful people,"[7] or in the words of St. Thomas Aquinas, for man who does not have "life that shall not end, in our true native land"[8] with Christ, who by his own death has broken down the wall of partition that separates one group from another. (Eph. 2:11-22)

[7] "Prayer of Thanksgiving," *Book of Common Prayer.*
[8] No. 209, Episcopal hymnal, 1940.

CHAPTER 8

Tragedy of Racially Divided Society

Difficulties with Research into Human Relations Problems

In Colombo, Ceylon, I was shown an elaborate model of a dam engineers were using to study every imaginable problem of water power in order to arrive at the soundest possible specifications for the next dam to be constructed. How wonderful it would be, I thought, if a similar sort of experiment could be conducted for human or social engineering. (I was visiting Ceylon as a consultant to the National Christian Council of Ceylon to study what the Christian community there could do in the face of the crisis caused by the Sinhalese-Tamil conflict.)

Experiment upon hypotheses under laboratory conditions is one of the standard methods of scientific research in every area except where human personalities are involved. In dealing with these problems—including inter-group tensions and their effects upon people involved—all we can do is to take each and every instance as it occurs, and study it for its own sake, or on its own merit. Every situation is unique when humanity is involved for the simple reason that every human personality is unique. What the German calls *Einmaligkeit*[1] is the essence of human events and we must never forget it. At the same time it is also true that by thoroughly understanding one particular event we may gain insights into something of the *universal* principle. What we need therefore is somehow to turn our own experiences into an experiment or make use of an event in which we are personally involved, as a laboratory.

This of course is not as easy as one may think at first; it certainly is far easier said than done. For one thing, it requires of us a high degree of objectivity, or detachment, to look at ourselves as if *we* were external objects. At the same time, the situation demands an equally intense sense of subjectivity, or involvement, to look at other people as if *they* were *we*. Such a combination is exceedingly difficult to achieve, for it is not only a matter of mind but also of heart. It requires an "informed heart," as the title of one of Dr. Bruno Bettelheim's books suggests, as well as a sharp mind.[2] In dealing with the problem of race relations, it also requires a "desegregated heart," as Mrs. Sarah Patton Boyle has called her book, as well as an unprejudiced mind.[3] With Kierkegaard we must acknowledge that "truth is subjectivity,"[4] when we deal with human events. And finally we must accept in humility and with determination that after all we who are involved and are involving others in a given situation are the ones who have to face up to it.

1 Happening-but-once-ness.

2 Bettelheim, B. *The Informed Heart: The human condition in mass society*. Glencoe: The Free Press; London: Thames & Hudson, 1960.

3 Boyle, S. P. *The Desegregated Heart: a Virginian's stand in time of transition*. New York: William Morrow & Co., 1962.

4 *Unscientific Postscript,* tr. by David F. Swenson and Walter Lowrie. Princeton: University Press, 1944.

No expert from outside alone can solve the problem for us.

How pertinent all this is became very clear when I sought to analyze why we the Christians of this generation have failed so miserably in coming to terms with the race problem. We, who belong to the world wide community of the faithful, transcending all racial, ethnic, national, and class distinctions, should not only have been free from racial tensions among ourselves (within the church), but also able to help our fellow men outside the church to overcome such tensions as those in which they have been caught up. We have to admit how miserably we have failed on both accounts. (The preceding chapters are largely a description of this failure.) Now we must try to understand why we have failed, and for this purpose, having no hypothesis to prove in any laboratory, I shall try to draw some generalizations from analyses of a couple of live situations.

Japanese American Relocation Center

In 1942-43 I found myself in one of the ten "relocation centers" along with many other people of Japanese origin. A great majority were U.S. citizens by virtue of birth in this country. The center was operated by the National War Relocation Authority, created by an executive order of the U.S. President, for the express purpose of: (1) "protective custody" of the people of Japanese descent loyal to this country from all forms of possible attack by American people under war-time hysteria and (2) "prevention of sabotage" by people of Japanese descent who might have been more loyal to Japan than to this country.

The center in which I spent one whole year had a population of 150,000, mostly from farming communities in the states of California, Oregon, and Washington, and was located in the middle of a sea of sagebrush beside the highway which connected Reno, Nevada, and Klamath Falls, Oregon. The center itself was in California near the Oregon border. Here we were separated from the world outside by the barbed wire fences around us and the network of bureaucratic red tape placing us simultaneously under the jurisdictions of U.S. Departments of War, Navy, Justice, and Interior. Gates were guarded by military sentries. The internal life of the center as well as the liaison with the world outside were administered by a body of appointed personnel with one called "Project Director" at the helm.

The official policy by directive from Washington was that of no fraternization between the administration and the evacuees. Here we were in a place which was as close to being a sociological laboratory to study the problems of human relationships as any society has ever seen. Sure enough, a community analyst was placed in all the centers, one of whom, Dr. Alexander Leighton, later published his study *The Governing of Men,*[5] which I understand was used as a text book by the Allied Occupation Authorities in developing their occupation policy in Japan. I had the good fortune of associating with Dr. Marvin Opler, an able anthropologist, who as a community analyst helped me to understand what was happening to people individually and collectively in the center.

Here, then, we have a controlled situation—a community of 150,000 people of one ethnic origin, herded into a re-

[5] Leighton, Alexander H., *The Governing of Men: General Principles and Recommendations Based on Experience at a Japanese Relocation Camp*. Princeton: University Press, 1945.

stricted area, to be governed by a group of another race. What happened to people on this artificially created "island" in the sea of sagebrush? Several things of interest to us may be briefly stated.

1. Tensions developed within the evacuee community.

a) It became apparent very soon after the center was established that there existed marked differences between the Japanese communities in California and in the Pacific Northwest (Oregon and Washington) in terms of outlook on the general American public, of first-hand experience in dealing and associating with Caucasian Americans, of children's school experience, etc.

b) There existed a tremendous conflict between generations in point of culture, mores, and languages. Difference of generation coincided with the difference in citizenship. The older generation, the immigrant from Japan, commonly called *Issei* (meaning "first generation" Japanese in the U.S.A.) were Japanese nationals, having been barred from naturalization by the Oriental Exclusion Act of 1924, and in many ways much more "Japanese" than the Japanese people in Japan. On the other hand, their children—U.S. citizens by virtue of their birth in this country, commonly called *Nisei* (literally "second generation")—were self-consciously more American than most other Americans, in that they had been trying to be accepted as Americans, oftentimes even by deliberately turning their back on anything Japanese, including the language. There was a third group, known within the Japanese community in this country as *Kibei* (meaning those who, born in the U.S.A., were reared in Japan and "returned to U.S.A."), who were mostly in their twenties then. Many of them were educated in Japan in the 1930's, at the height of the jingoistic nationalism of the military-controlled Japan, and came back belligerently pro-Japan, speaking English with a marked Japanese accent. They did not fit either in the *Issei* circle or in the *Nisei* circle.

c) Within all these sub-groups, there were Christians, Buddhists, and agnostics.

d) Although the majority were farmers, there were an appreciable number of professional people: physicians, dentists, lawyers, businessmen, university professors, etc. Rural folk and city people made another subdivision within the evacuee community.

Under more normal circumstances these differences had been neither manifest nor strongly felt. People had freely associated with one another across the borders before they were put in the center. Within the center it looked as though everybody was marked with a label indicating which group he belonged to. It was assumed that a man's group determined his opinion, position, or attitude, with regard to every issue that had any bearing whatsoever on the welfare of the evacuees. There was a strong tendency to divide people between *pro* and *con* on anything: one was assumed to be either pro-America or anti-America, either pro- or anti-administration; pro- or anti-Japan; pro- or anti-resettlement outside of the center, etc., depending on which group(s) one was identified with. The individuality of each person was lost and independent thinking by individual persons was replaced by collective mentality of groups.

2. The evacuee community soon became a rumor-ridden community.

Cynicism toward truths or toward sincerity of other people, on one hand, and gullibility toward half-truths or unfounded gossips, on the other, went hand in hand. It was as if they were saying, "We can no longer believe in anybody who claims to be sincere and anything which claims to be true. But we can no longer be absolutely sure that things reported, however ridiculous or fantastic they may be, are untrue, either." People consequently believed what they wanted to believe and rejected everything which they did not want to believe. Like the one who is reported to have said, "My mind is made up; don't confuse me with facts," the evacuees in the relocation center did not want to have truths disturb their minds. So the *Issei* believed a completely unfounded rumor that the Japanese navy had sunk the whole U.S. fleet; *Kibei* believed that the white Americans molested *Nisei* co-eds; the *Nisei* believed that farmers in California were making a fortune on what the Japanese had to leave behind, etc. Being cut off from the general stream of American life, the evacuees were in no position to check the source or verify the authenticity of everything that reached their ears.

3. The relocation center became a hopelessly demoralizing environment for all the evacuees, male and female, old and young, Christian and Buddhist, alike.

It was a collective society, in the governing of which none of them had any part whatsoever. There was little room for personal incentive to improve their lot. All the plans a group of them might have made could be dismissed as useless by the administration. There was no possibility of earning wages commensurate to one's skill or industry. Children saw their parents "loafing" every day and learned to be "independent" of them. For both parents and children were wards of the government and children knew that their well-being was no longer dependent on their parents' hard work and loving care. Thus parents lost moral control over their children, and children lost respect for their parents. This was a terrible blow to the Japanese family and its demoralizing effect upon the whole community was quite evident. Petty crimes, promiscuity, gambling, cheating, etc., increased among all age levels. Japanese people who had been reputed to be hard-working, family-centered, honest, and clean, were on the way toward a serious state of moral degradation or spiritual disintegration.

4. Race relations were *ipso facto* something of caste relations.

To be of Japanese descent automatically meant to be governed, and to be of Caucasian background, to govern. No amount of knowledge, skill, experience, university degree, and even wealth could change the status thus determined by race. Numerically the evacuees far outnumbered the administration, but in terms of power the administration was in the absolute majority. To have one racial group of numerical minority rule with absolute power over the numerical majority of another race—this was precisely the pattern of race relations in the relocation center. The inevitable consequence was the breakdown, or utter absence, of communication between the two racial groups. The administration was motivated by genuine good-will toward, and profound concern for, the evacuees and their welfare.

But this was not understood or accepted by the evacuee community at all. In the eyes of the evacuees the administration was the U.S. Government written small, and as such stood for all the ills that had fallen upon them through evacuation: their economic loss, white people's hostility toward them as epitomized by the activities of such groups as Native Sons of Golden West, California Vegetable and Fruits Growers Association, etc.; Lt. Gen. DeWitt who had once made a public statement, "Once a Jap, always a Jap;" and all the rest. There was a fence within the relocation center that divided the residential area of the appointed personnel from the evacuees, but even without it the two groups would not have met face to face, for they were completely polarized one from the other.

5. What happened to West Coast society after Japanese American evacuation?

I add here a brief word on what happened to the West Coast society after all the people of Japanese descent had been removed from their midst. Contrary to the old proverb, "out of sight, out of mind," people began to be more and more preoccupied with Japanese, and having no Japanese person in the flesh and blood living among them, whom they could see, talk to and listen to, they began to develop images of Japanese. Any resemblance between their images and a living Japanese was purely coincidental. The life inside the relocation centers was talked about as if it were of strange people in a strange land. Many an ungrounded rumor about what the War Relocation Authority was doing in the relocation centers was spread far and wide. Putting us out of sight did not seem to make Americans on the Pacific Coast any the less hysterical.

TRAGEDY OF RACIALLY DIVIDED SOCIETY

What can be done in such a situation? How can the problems created by the center be solved?

Now with these five points in mind I want you, my reader, successively to place yourself in the place of the director of the camp, of one of the Japanese pastors, and of the U.S. congressman from one of the West Coast states. Assuming that you are a convinced and committed Christian, a patriotic (in the truest and the highest sense of the term) American and a man of rational mind, I want you to think what you would have done and what sort of results you could have expected from your action. I would be astonished if you could do anything of real significance without tampering with the structure of the relocation center itself. Ultimate solution could not have been possible short of the dissolution or liquidation of the center itself. As long as the center was in operation, the best policy of the director could not be put into effect because the evacuee community would not believe in his integrity. The best sermon on love preached by the pastor could not persuade his listeners. They would doubt seriously how the kind of people responsible for their mass evacuation or life in the relocation center could ever receive their love and respond to it. All the congressional investigations could not communicate the true state of affairs in the center to an electorate so pathologically preoccupied with the so-called Japanese problem. As long as you, as a member of one racial group, can do no more than to think of, talk about, hear about, and even pray for members of another racial group without ever sitting down with them, having conversation with them and together kneeling before God to pray for one another, with all the good-will in the world you can do very little to serve the true needs of the people you want to serve.

The only thing that could be done, as long as we were detained in the relocation center, was for some of us to become "law-breakers," or to put it less shockingly, to break man-made laws in order to obey God's laws. Fortunately, there were enough men and women on both sides who were Christian enough to forget their race, their status, and even the administrative directive and begin to be friends with one another. In this venture, Director Elmer Shirrell and his wife Eleanor were the first ones on one side and several Christian leaders, both clerical and lay, were the first ones on the other. The core of people thus brought together into a supra-racial Christian fellowship became the well-spring of sanity within that community which otherwise was rapidly turning into a pathologically introverted community.

Ceylon Under Emergency

CEYLON 1948-1956

For the second case study I take you to Ceylon, 1961. Ceylon became independent in 1948 almost as a by-product of India's independence. There had been agitation for national independence earlier which, led by the English-educated elite, was inspired by the independence movement in India. As far as the Ceylonese masses were concerned, they had never been involved in any real struggle for freedom as Indians had, or as Africans are now having to go through. In 1948 the British handed the government over to the United National Party which was made up of highly trained leaders of all ethnic groups, Sinhalese, Tamil, and Burgher. They were all the so-called "English-educated" and thought very much as Englishmen did. It was a peaceful transition of power from the colonial to the indigenous government and the British were absolutely confident that of all their colonies Ceylon had been best prepared for independence.

In 1956 the late S.W.R.D. Bandaranaike, an Oxford-educated intellectual of aristocratic origin, having renounced his religious affiliation as an Anglican, identified himself as a Buddhist and formed a new political party, Sri Lanka Freedom Party (SLFP). He won victory in the general election to form a cabinet, on the platform that Buddhism be the national religion of Ceylon and Sinhala her official language. The platform may have been no more than a political gimmick on his part but he was astonished by the response of the *swabasha* (meaning "vernacular-speaking") Sinhalese Buddhist masses. He found himself a captive of his own party platform!

CEYLON 1956-61

Buddhist monks who had a tremendous influence upon the Sinhalese masses kept on pressing Bandaranaike's government to implement its pronounced policy and agitated the masses to demonstrate their strength. The emergency of 1958—mass massacre of Tamil people by Sinhalese people; later, assassination of Bandaranaike himself, and subsequent establishment of a virtual dictatorship by SLFP—threw Ceylon into a turmoil. The Tamils who are Dravidian-speaking Hindus and are in a numerical minority, and the Sinhalese who are Aryan-speaking Buddhists and are in the majority, stood against each other, while the Burghers, descendants of Eurasian background, who are mostly Christians, were made to feel that there was no place for them in Ceylon under the SLFP government and many of them emigrated to Australia.

Early in 1961 the Ceylon Tamils, led by a devoutly Christian layman, Mr. S. J. V. Chelvanayakam, put on a nation-wide *Satyagraha* campaign (Gandhian type of non-violent demonstration) of non-cooperation with the government in power. As a result, the relationships between the Sinhalese and the Tamils were deteriorating badly.

CHRISTIAN ACTIONS

The National Christian Council through its Study Center (Dr. Basil Jackson, Director) had continually studied the problem from the Christian standpoint. It appealed to both the government and the Sinhalese public to be fair and just to the Tamils and other minority groups, and to the Tamils not to lose their head and do anything hasty. In the midst of the Satyagraha campaign, a study conference on "Christian Witness in Contemporary Ceylon" was held at the Uduvil Girls' College in Jaffna,[6] under the leadership of Dr. D. T. Niles and under the auspices of the East Asia Christian Conference Committee on Church and Society, which a goodly number of Sinhalese Christians from other parts of Ceylon attended as a matter of course.[7] At the beginning of the campaign, shortly after the government had declared an emergency, a delegation of Sinhalese Christians led by Archdeacon Harold de Soyso of Co-

[6] Jaffna is the stronghold of Tamil people.

[7] This required more courage than one can appreciate outside Ceylon.

lombo paid a good-will visit to the Jaffna district. The Study Center organ, the *Christian News Bulletin*, had since 1956 said practically all that needed to be said on every aspect of the problem, openly and objectively, in season and out of season, urging all segments of the Ceylonese society to act rationally. This is one of the most courageous pieces of Christian journalism I have so far personally encountered. All in all, the Christian community in Ceylon, involving members of all ethnic communities though in a terribly small minority (Roman Catholics 9 per cent, Protestant 1 per cent of the total population), had been taking a straightforward stand, raising a clear voice against all manners of injustice found in any quarter.

The situation was not improving at all in the summer of 1961, emergency had not been lifted, and the hostility between Sinhalese and Tamil groups was growing more intense as time went by. It was at this juncture that I was invited to visit Ceylon. At the center of my concern was the question: What more or what else should the Christian community in Ceylon do to put an end to the communal tensions in their country?[8]

What has been happening to Ceylon since her independence may be summarized as follows:

1. Ceylonese nationalism up to, and at the time of, inde-

[8] I spent six intensive weeks reading all sorts of things, having interviews, conferences, consultations, both talking with and listening to all sorts of people—the governor, several cabinet ministers, leaders of Tamil political party, leaders of the Socialist party (known as LSSP), social scientists, historians, lawyers, doctors, Christian ministers, Buddhist priests, Hindu philosophers, labor union organizers, school teachers, housewives, civil servants, missionaries, students, and university professors—Tamils, Sinhalese, Burghers, members of Muslim Community—traveling from one place to another between Colombo and Jaffna.

pendence was a genuinely transcommunal movement, led and supported largely by the English-educated Tamils, Sinhalese, and Burghers. They were thoroughly westernized in their thought pattern but constituted only 5 per cent of the total population. They were patriotic nationalists but their concept of the nation was not a bit different from that of the British colonial government in the eyes of the *swabasha* masses, especially Buddhist Sinhalese. There was thus a gradual rise of protest among the *sarong*-wearing[9] Sinhalese masses, which one may identify as a revolt of masses against the oligarchy of the westernized elite.

2. The Buddhist Sinhalese masses, once in power, are in need of an image of Ceylon as an autonomous nation with her own identity and integrity—a Ceylon which is different either from Britain or from India, or from any other nation in the East or in the West. The easiest way to achieve this was deemed to make of Ceylon a Sinhala-speaking, Buddhist nation, though at the expense of Tamil people. And this the government in power has been trying to do in the shortest possible space of time.

3. The Tamil people, who for two thousand years have made Ceylon their home and have substantially contributed to the independence of Ceylon, naturally enough feel that the Sinhalese people have betrayed their trust. The Tamils, too, want to maintain their cultural integrity and ethnic identity, which they are made to feel the Sinhalese are deliberately trying to annihilate. Tamils are perfectly willing to learn Sinhala since it is the language of the majority and

[9] Generally speaking men who wear trousers are English-speaking while those clad in *sarong* (native man's clothes) are *swabasha,* or vernacular-speaking.

they are shrewd enough to recognize it to be to their own advantage to know the language of the people among whom they live and with whom they trade, but the moment it is laid down by law they are required to use Sinhala in order to be first-class citizens, they rebel and quite justifiably, too.

4. The Tamils are a minority in Ceylon (approximately 2 million Tamils against 6 million Sinhalese). They are, however, much feared by the Sinhalese because across the channel there are 40 million Tamils in South India. Moreover, the Tamils have always honored their own language, and educated Tamils in Ceylon are without exception bilingual (Tamil and English) and they keep up with modern Tamil literature, art, philosophy through newspapers, cultural magazines, scholarly journals and books published in India.

In contrast to this, Sinhalese have neglected their language for many generations. In 1904 one of the greatest Ceylonese statesmen, Sir Ponnambalam Ramanathan (a Tamil), spoke at Ananda College in Colombo to Sinhalese Buddhist students on the use of the Sinhala language, saying in part: "If the Sinhalese lips will not speak the Sinhala language, who else is there to speak it? . . . If those of you who are considered leading men and women of the country do not cultivate your language and make it a vehicle in ordinary use for good thoughts it will live in the lips of the illiterate only, with the result that it will become more and more neglected and corrupted, at last die an unwept death."[10] This warning, uttered by a Tamil man more than

[10] From *T. L. R. Leaflet* No. 10, published by the League for the Promotion of Tamil Language Rights.

half a century ago, had gone unheeded by educated Sinhalese until it was almost too late.

Now the Sinhalese nationalists are worried because Sinhala is spoken only in Ceylon. Should six million Sinhalese be swallowed up by forty million Tamils from across the channel, Sinhala language and Sinhalese culture will be lost forever. There is a sense in which the Sinhalese community, though in the numerical majority, suffers from a minority complex and culturally from an inferiority complex, in the face of the vitality of the Tamil community. This makes the Sinhalese people become more belligerent in their effort to enforce the "Sinhala Only" policy among the Tamils.

5. At the level of personal relationships, Tamil and Sinhalese people are just as friendly as can be. (To an outsider it is hardly possible to distinguish one from the other.) But, the political situation and the resultant social climate being what they are, people are extremely conscious of their being either Tamil or Sinhalese, which inevitably conditions their outlook on one another. Under such circumstances even the friendliest relationships between personal friends tend to be somewhat strained. Within the Christian community, however, the majority being English-educated, there is very little problem between the two ethnic groups.

6. The most serious problem, as far as my personal observation goes, is the almost unbridgeable gulf that exists between the English-educated elite, including all communities (although no more than 5 per cent of the total population), and the *sarong*-wearing, *swabasha* Buddhist Sinhalese who constitute the absolute majority and dominate the nation's politics today. Integration of all ethnic (which cor-

responds to religio-cultural, too) groups to make of them one Ceylonese nation has so far been conceived of only by the English-educated, and in highly westernized terms. This is not understood or appreciated by the masses at all—in fact, it is rebelled against by them violently.

On the other hand, the image of Ceylon presented by the *swabasha* masses is to the English-educated so crude that it is utterly unacceptable. And, between them there exists a language difficulty almost as serious as between say Americans and Japanese in Japan! Consequently there has been no real dialogue within the Sinhalese community between the English-educated and the *swabasha* groups. In fact the English-educated have permitted themselves to be politically pushed around by the *swabasha* people lest their support should be lost at the next general election.

Since 1956 the *swabasha* people have regained their self-respect and dignity, and the tide cannot be turned. This probably is the hardest thing for most of the Ceylonese Christians to come to terms with.

7. All in all, Ceylon in 1961 was a society under one national flag but split into several ethno-cultural, religio-linguistic communities, among whom communication hardly existed. Like the Gerasene demoniac, the name for Ceylon in 1961 was "legion, for they were many." (Mark 5:1-9) Ceylon, furthermore, is an island nation and in spite of the air travel and radio communication, she can be pretty isolated from the rest of the world. Like the relocation center situated as an island in the middle of an ocean of sagebrush, Ceylon as I saw her was a pathologically introverted society. There every group was looking at everything only from its own vantage point, with the result that every

group became a problem to every other group!—each talking always *about* but never *with* the other. Tamil men who dared to associate with Sinhalese men and vice versa were more often than not suspected by both their own people and the people of the other community. This might be the predicament in which the Christian community as a whole found itself: it was discredited by both Sinhalese and Tamil communities.

These seven points I have listed above were not terribly difficult for anybody who came from outside to see, but were hidden to many otherwise intelligent Ceylonese people, simply because they had been subjectively involved in what to each person was a life-and-death struggle. Given those conditions, all the pronouncements of the National Christian Council, all the analyses made by the Study Center and published in the *Christian News Bulletin,* all the direct appeals to the Government repeatedly made by officially appointed spokesmen of the Christian community, all the sermons preached from the pulpit, and all the gestures of good-will made by men and women in the pews towards those of the opposite community—all had proved almost entirely in vain. Among Christians of all ethnic communities there has been no dearth of good-will, courage, and willingness to witness, and many acts of heroism could be recounted.

Still the fact remains that not much of anything that really counts seems to have happened. Without being judgmental I venture to suggest what I think is the reason: It is because neither the Christian community corporately nor Christian people individually made a serious attempt to build a proper framework within which contact and communication between communities at odds against each other can take place. The framework I am speaking of is both conceptual and institutional. One without the other will not do much good. This will be the subject matter of the next chapter.

To conclude this chapter it may suffice to reiterate that to segregate an ethnic or racial group is no solution where the problem of ethnic tensions is acute; on the contrary segregation rather intensifies the tensions. Furthermore, to be preoccupied with problems of one society in isolation from the world around it only contributes to magnify the differences that exist among various groups. Both the Japanese relocation center in the U.S.A. (1942-45) and Ceylon (1956-61) demonstrate more acutely what is in less degree quite commonplace here in the U.S.A. and elsewhere in the world. Most of our trouble comes from our unwillingness to face up to the fact that people who are of different racial backgrounds than our own are among us to stay and they are given by God to us as our neighbors. Also, because we are too pathologically concerned about ourselves, we jump to the conclusion that their presence in our proximity will inevitably result in their invasion into the private domain of our life.

In this respect, Christians—a great majority of them at any rate—have not been doing much better than others. In terms of organized action and practice, the Christian churches in general have been no better if not much worse than the trade unions, industrial and commercial firms, national and state governments and their related agencies. This should not surprise us, for in this country churches and all these other groups are pretty much made up of the same people.

Christians as individual citizens and churches as organized institutions both have failed in solving the problem of tensions among different racial and ethnic groups chiefly because they too have been estranged from God and have lost the vantage point from which they should have been enabled to look at every human being as their God-given neighbor, nothing more, nothing less. Christians thus estranged from God cannot but conform to the world, and conforming to the world they have lost power to transform it. Churches so preoccupied with their institutional well-being cannot but fail to *be the church* in the world for its redemption.

CHAPTER 9

The Church's Mission in an Emerging One World

Weakness of Christian Approach in the Past

By now it has become convincingly clear, I trust, that neither race *per se* nor social difference is the root of the race problem. The real problem is *what people think* race is. Furthermore it is not what people individually think, but what I have earlier called a "collective mentality"—the judgment of one group imposed upon another—that is the root of our problem. *Scientific exposition* helps to enlighten people individually by replacing misinformation with correct information. It may even lead them to change their opinions on what race is. But seldom does knowledge of this sort make a dent on the collective mentality of a group. Collective mentality defies reason.

By the same token, *moral exhortation* has not proved very effective. The injunction, "Love your neighbor" is always countered by the question, "Who is my neighbor?" which betrays the determined unwillingness to do what is both understood and believed to be right and therefore ought to be done. (Luke 10:25-29) Faced by the exhortation that one ought to be just and fair in one's relationships with people of different racial background, one can always construe "justice" in such a way as to rationalize all manner of discriminatory practices: e.g., "This is what is best for them," or "This is exactly what *they* want or need," assuming that *they* are so different from *us* that to think of them in exactly the same way as we think of ourselves is doing an injustice to them! This assumption is usually rooted in the collective mentality of the group to which one belongs.

Personal contact by which we know people as individuals has likewise proved effective only in limited ways. In the first place, people who are thoroughly conditioned or "strait-jacketed" by the collective mentality of their own group do not want to meet people of another group on a personal basis. As the old saying goes, one can lead a horse to water but cannot make him drink. Unless somehow the desire to become involved with persons of different racial background is aroused in a man, interchange simply does not take place.[1]

Inherent Difficulties with Democracy

Finally, much of what is going on under the name of Christian or democratic *social action*, though by no means all of it, is more like an elaborately organized design by

[1] To arouse such a desire in people who have deep-seated racial prejudices, the church has usually appealed to their reason in terms of objective or scientific truth, or to their conscience in terms of moral imperative. There has been precious little result, except possibly to stiffen backs and reinforce existing racial resistance. Besides, if prejudiced people were compelled, by chance or by design, to meet persons of other racial backgrounds, they would not be open enough to get to know them personally and the result is often negative in that it confirms this prejudice.

which to induce or even trick otherwise unwilling people into doing what is objectively right but what they are not subjectively convinced is right. If people do what is good or right only under pressure of external authority, it is not good enough from the standpoint of Christianity. This does not mean, however, that no attempt should be made to enforce the society to do away with its long-established pattern of racial discrimination. This would be tantamount to *forcing* the Negro citizens to stay wronged and is obviously contradictory to true Christian and democratic principles. We must beware lest we should become so doctrinaire about our principles as to sacrifice people on the altar of our own opinions. We can be so firm in upholding the democratic principle that we may refuse to do anything while one group of people merrily continue to discriminate against another group of people, subjecting them to unjust sufferings. This is to condone racial discrimination in the name of democracy!

There is a danger inherent in many a Christian action and we must not be blind to it. For fear of this danger people often object to everything in which they detect any element of coercion, saying "Everything must happen naturally." They state the argument this way: For a person of one racial group to meet a person of another racial group and for them to get personally acquainted with each other —this must happen naturally, and must not be coerced, engineered, or legislated. Those who take this position are convinced that even peace, law and order, or justice—if achieved at the expense of freedom—will not be worth having. In terms of the absolute, they may be right,[2] but we

[2] I am not saying that they are absolutely right.

have not yet arrived in the realm of the absolute and therefore must find a way which is "the best possible" under given circumstances.

Faced with a critical or a potentially explosive situation, loaded with acute racial tensions, the church has usually failed to be effective largely because its leadership has not been able either to think and/or to act beyond appealing to people's reason or conscience (usually by way of pronouncement or position-taking statement). Moral exhortation to the effect that people of different racial groups should meet for Christian fellowship has not proved very effective, nor has social action program of one sort or another to translate the Christian teaching on race relations into practice. These are all laudable activities but not very effective for the simple reason that they do not take into account the basic nature of the race problem which, as we have seen in the preceding chapters, is basically a matter of inter-group rather than inter-personal relations, that is, dynamic interaction between groups with strong collective mentalities. (See Chapters 4 and 5.)

Heritage of Missionary Movement

Most of us contemporary Christians, and especially the Protestants in the West, fail to recognize this elemental fact about the race problem for two mutually related reasons. One reason is that our faith has been shaped by long involvement in the foreign missionary movement. The other is that the racial tensions have been chiefly, though by no manner or means exclusively, between the white men of Western Christendom and peoples of colored races whose conversion has been the object of foreign missionary movements. It is of crucial importance therefore that we understand something of the basic characteristics of the missionary movement itself, although space does not permit me to engage in a thoroughgoing critique of it from a combined standpoint of theology, history, and sociology.

To put it candidly, the modern missionary movement of Western Protestantism[3] was characterized by several features, of which an outstanding few may be listed as follows:

1. The driving force was the Pietist's encounter with the sinfulness (or the fallen nature) of humanity at the depth of his own inward experience. The miserable state of the "unconverted" Christian led him to relate himself to the even more miserable state of the heathen.

2. This made the missionary enterprise subjectivistic and individualistic in its ethos and basic orientation, with sole emphasis upon the state of the soul of the individual apart from everybody else and regardless of his social context. Each person, it was firmly believed, had to make a personal encounter at the depth of his "spiritual" life with Christ as his savior.

3. There was a tacit distinction made between evangelism and mission: *evangelism* was directed to the unconverted or uncommitted, nominal Christians, with revivalism as its main technique as well as its ultimate end; *mission* was directed to the heathen, and therefore it was virtually "foreign missions" with gathering of converts into a new branch of Christ's church as its basic method as well

[3] Pioneered by such people as Bartholomäus Ziegenbalg and his colleague Heinrich Plütschau of the Royal Danish Mission (dispatched from Halle University) to Tranquebar, India; John Eliot, among American Indians in the New England colony; William Carey, Adoniram Judson, etc.

as its ultimate end. In this country the missionary enterprises were first among the American Indians and later among Negro Americans and the Oriental immigrants. In all cases these efforts were carried out as if they were "foreign" missions though within the boundaries of the continental U.S.A. (Chapter 4) while evangelism by way of revivalism was seen mostly on the frontier among the pioneers.

4. The *leitmotif* of American missionary enterprise was inevitably the conquest of the unredeemed. Heathen, pagan, colored race, and foreign somehow became synonymous in the mind of the missionary and were regarded as things to be conquered. The founding fathers' vision of a biblical commonwealth to be established in New England became the standard by which all religions, cultures, and national heritages of people of colored races were to be judged. Mission came to mean:

a) to rescue individual persons out of all such foreign cultures, pagan religions, and heathenish superstitions and practices, and

b) to destroy all such religions and cultures.

Importance of Group for Man to Be Person

Even today we find ourselves more often than we suspect under the spell of this nineteenth century idea of mission when we think about the church's mission. The transition from "Church Missions" to "Church's Mission" does not seem to have run its full course yet. There is a sense in which the rise of Neo-Orthodoxy with its emphasis upon theological purity (whatever this may mean) has made the Christians in the West extremely fearful of religious syncretism in the non-Western world, and has revived the *conquest motif*. The ghost of the "foreign" missionary movement of the last century is still haunting us.

The subjective individualism infecting expressions of Christian faith makes us think of a person apart from the group(s) to which he belongs, which in fact is to treat him as something less than a person. The being of his person, i.e., his personality, is rooted in the group or groups of which he is an integral part. If we, in the name of individualism or personalism—however much rationalized in such terms as sanctity, dignity, and ultimacy of individual person—think of him, deal with him, and try to relate ourselves to him apart from his group(s), we are in effect seeing him in *abstract* or in a socio-cultural vacuum. He whom we are thus looking at is not his true and full self. To reduce a living person to an abstract image or little more than a "mental construct" is hardly a Christian act. This, however, is what our missionary movement has been doing by its emphasis on saving the soul of each pagan in isolation from his *habitat,* i.e., the historical, socio-cultural context embodied in the groups of which his entire life is an integral part. To relate oneself *Christianly* to another person, be he a Christian or something else, requires accepting him *as he is rooted* in his nation, his race, his culture, his family, his peer group, etc., etc.

If man were living in a static society of homogeneous composition, the group *per se* would not be a problem, for in effect everybody would belong to one and the same group—one big group which was coterminal with the *universe* which everybody shared. The real-life situation is quite different. Ours is an increasingly dynamic world in which, on the one hand, a "one world community" is emerging, and on the other hand, every local community is becoming more and more heterogeneous in composition. As the whole world turns into a neighborhood, every neighborhood turns into a little world. (See Chapter 6.)

In the context of such a contemporary world situation the meaning of groups looms large—groups readily identifiable by their visible or physical characteristics; groups predetermined by nature (i.e., biologically) for one to be born into or belong to; groups that have historically developed and become "internal environments" of their members; and groups to which man chooses to belong, etc. In a *mass society,* which the urban-technological civilization inevitably brings about, all these groups play far more serious roles than we have so far recognized, in shaping man's personality, his outlook on life, way of thinking, manner in which he relates or fails to relate to others. (See Chapter 7.)

The Church's Mission in Relation to Groups

In the light of such an understanding of the dynamic interaction of human groups within the context of modern mass society, what do we have to say about the mission of the church in the area of race relations? In this area, of all areas, the church must take the group very seriously. To fail to do so, as we have seen, has in fact been the basic cause for the ineffectiveness of the church's witness. There is a sense in which the church's witness in relation to the race problem is nothing other than the church's mission to modern man who, having been hopelessly lost in the wilderness of mass society, is desperately trying to assert his self-identity in terms of his membership in one group or another. It is group, not race, that is of primary importance. (See Chapter 7.) To say this, however, is not to magnify group or absolutize it, but to insist on seeing man in terms of his group and in the context of dynamic interaction between his group and others in the society.

This means that one can hardly conceive of the church's mission to man in the modern mass society apart from clarifying the meaning of human groups in the light of the gospel. Proclamation of the gospel is not so much persuading non-Christians to become Christians (i.e., to forsake their allegiance to any other religions and to adhere to the Christian religion) as bringing into light God's will which has so far been hidden within, though always underlying, standing behind, or running through, the history of all human groups.

To illustrate, and speaking specifically, the church's mission to a Negro American is to help him answer the question: "What does it mean for me to be a Negro in the U.S.A. today?" This is a prerequisite to answering the ultimate question: "Who am I?" For as long as he evades this question, the Negro American will not find his salvation. The ethnic group to which he has been destined to belong is that with which others for good or for ill identify him, and which, if he fails to, or refuses to, accept as his own identity, will forever remain the source of self-hate and psychic torment in him.

At the same time, the white American will not find his salvation until he, among other things, accepts the Negro American unqualifiedly as a person; that is, until he has a hand in making it possible for every Negro American to be justly proud of his ethnic origin and background.

This requires a full emancipation of the white American from his race prejudice against the Negro and all other ethnic groups. Such emancipation is impossible apart from a profound understanding of the meaning of ethnic groups at this stage of human history in the light of the gospel. The church's task is thus intensely theological.

Nationalism of New Nations

By the same token, the racial issues in the international relations between the West and the emerging new nations demands the church's attention. These nations, with all their handicaps, shortcomings, and defects in every imaginable aspect of their life, constitute the groups which give identity to those who belong to them. For example, one who up till now has been known only as *African* (to my mind comes that most telling title of James Baldwin's recent book: *Nobody Knows My Name*) will from now on identify himself with his nation as a Nigerian, Ghanian, Sierra Leonian, Cameroonian, Liberian, etc. This is to assert one's identity in terms of the group to which one belongs, to take pride in and take seriously the soil in which one's personality has its root.

As the missionary movement awakened in the people of Africa a new dimension of their own human dignity, and then somehow thwarted it (see Chapter 2), so the colonial rule has made this phenomenon of African nationalism and personality both possible and impossible:

possible, because it was the colonial rule that has by force so consolidated many tribal solidarities as to lay the foundation of modern national states;

impossible, because it has by force kept the emerging nations under its rule, whether race prejudice has played any decisive role in this or not.

Emancipated from the yoke of their own tribalism, the indigenous people of Africa are now finding nations more relevant symbols for self-identification than tribes, continents, or even race. To assert their national identity is to be free from the yokes of their old tribalism. Thus conceived, in their nationalism is their positive acceptance of this newly acquired identity and dignity of their own personality, while forces of rapid social change are throwing them into a worldwide ocean of mass society with increasing emphasis on depersonalization of individuals.

Nationalism in the wake of decolonization is, however, loaded with varieties of destructive forces. Racism in terms of hostility bred by hostility is one of the most dangerous among such forces. As a renowned Indian Christian thinker, Sri M. M. Thomas, says, nationalism in the newly emerging Afro-Asian countries is *at once* a legacy of, and a reaction against, the Western imperialism. Insofar as it is a reaction against the Western colonial powers, it is bound to have a strong element of anti-Westernism and anti-white racism. This is inevitable and to expect them to be entirely free from it is to forget the historical fact that theirs is a counter-racism reacting against the racism of the "white" world. Here the *ministry of reconciliation* is inseparable from the *redemption of history,* in which *forgiveness* between groups must be conceived as a love-creating and community-binding power, not as a passive virtue but a dynamic power. Asking their forgiveness of our past racism and forgiving them their present counter-racism, we must *Christianly* accept their nationalism and relate ourselves to them in terms of their new national identities. Here again the task is intensely theological.

Reconciliation Between Groups

What I have so far said must not be construed to mean the task is one exclusively for the white Protestant Christian in the West, relating to the rest of mankind. It goes without saying that inter-group relations, Christianly conceived, must be a two-way proposition. Reconciliation between groups means establishment or restoration of such two-way relationships in place of various forms of majority-minority power relations, not annihilation of groups or interaction between groups. Society that comes into being as a result of such reconciliation between groups is precisely what we mean by an integrated society.

Thus conceived, the emerging society of mankind is bound to be characterized by its ethno-cultural pluralism both at the global level as one world community and at the local level as a microcosmic society. The oneness will not be achieved by way of amalgamation or assimilation, as it was once believed by advocates of the "melting-pot" theory, but by way of positive inter-relationships between a number of groups, each retaining its own unique identity. A racially integrated society in our sense is one in which racial or ethnic communities may maintain their group identities without ever being closed communities. It is a society in which, for example, a Japanese person who fulfills his manhood as a Japanese is capable of accepting, and being accepted by, an American who likewise has grown mature enough to accept a Japanese as a person without expecting him to become an American. This is the kind of positive relationship that ought to exist between all ethno-cultural groups in a truly integrated society.

Integrated society is a society in which positive acceptance of group identities by all enables everybody to be such a fully integrated person that he can relate himself to all others whose ethno-cultural backgrounds are radically different from his own. It is a society in which interracial marriage ceases to be a social issue. We Christians believe that such a society is entirely achievable because we know that we all share in one common humanity, while each of us belongs to one or more ethno-cultural groups.

Integration then is not something we who believe in racial equality have to work to bring about, but it is something which has been taking place and will continue to take place whether or not anybody likes it. We can either accept it or resist it—by accepting it we shall live contemporaneously in and with the emerging one world community, whereas by resisting it we shall be only trying to live in the bygone past and obstructing the realization of the one world community as well as making our own lives miserable. "I call heaven and earth to witness against you this day," says the Book of Deuteronomy, in the name of God, at one of the most crucial points of transition in the history of Israel, "that I have set before you life and death, blessing and curse; therefore choose life, that you and your descendants may live." (Deut. 30:19)

Christian Mission Reconsidered

We of this generation have to grow out of the nineteenth century concept of mission, according to which mission meant the conversion of heathen lands by so-called Christian nations. Through the worldwide missionary movement the church of Christ has by now been planted in every known nation of the world leaving literally no heathen land as such. Furthermore, the Bible witnesses to the fact that "God in Christ *has reconciled* the world to himself." Now the church in which the Kingship of Christ is recognized and magnified must work in the world which though redeemed by Christ has not acknowledged the Kingship of Christ. This is the mission of the church and there is no other.

To put the church and the world thus in antithesis to each other, however, is misleading. Empirically at least, the church is in the world and the world is in the church. The two are not segregated from but intertwined with each other. The world constitutes the context in which the church is to be the church, and the church is charged by God to be the "soul of the world," and between the two there exist tensions all the time.

To put it more sociologically, the church must maintain its own integrity, as it relates itself to the world which has its own integrity. Although the two are inseparably interpenetrated, the church is not a part of the world set aside for something specific called religion nor is the world a secularized church. Each has its own identity and yet the two are not segregated one from the other—there is no *apartheid* between them. The church's mission is to be the church, that is, to assert her identity and maintain her integrity, neither in isolation from nor in opposition to, but within the context of and in relation to the world.

To translate this thesis into practical terms of race relations, the real tension is not between the white and the colored races, nor between the dominant and subordinate groups, but between the community of the baptized and that of the unbaptized; the baptized are those who, having once lost their identity rooted in all sorts of human groups, have regained a new identity rooted in the God-given community in which "there is neither Jew nor Greek, neither bond nor free, neither male nor female."

This must not be construed to mean that the tension is between the *integrationists* (so-called) and the *segregationists* (so-called), nor between the *liberal* (so-called) and the *conservative* (or reactionary) (so-called). (I add "so-called" each time advisedly.) In a very profound sense, here, too, integration is already taking place, for the white race is inextricably involved in the colored races and vice versa, though each has not lost its own group identity. To think that segregation of one from the other is possible is as much a folly as to think it possible to take a pound of living flesh without shedding blood at all (cf., Shakespeare's *Merchant of Venice*).

Church's Mission Re: Race Relations

What, then, is the unique contribution of the church in the area of race relations, among the contributions of the government, the university and other research institutes, the professional agencies engaged in race relations (sometimes called more inclusively human relations), and so on? Again the answer is, "Let the church be the church"—reconciling and forgiving in the context of a world torn into pieces by all sorts of devisive forces, among which *racism is one of the most formidable.*

The church's mission in such a world is to proclaim the

gospel of reconciliation in specific reference to its disintegration caused by racial tensions and conflicts. The internal disintegration of the world has been recognized in such terms as the breakdown of traditional morality and social structures; group antagonisms, racial and otherwise ("wars and rumors of wars"); phenomenal increase of mental disorders (alcoholism, neuropsychosis, suicide, etc.); and disintegration of family life (divorce, juvenile delinquency, promiscuity, etc.). All these are symptoms of the basic illness of human society which has been estranged from God and from its own self. In such a situation the most pressing missionary task of the church is for her to be an integrating community[4] within the distintegrating world. And it is in this respect that the church has to speak to the world on the meaning of various types of human groups, such as nations and ethno-cultural groups, within the framework of divine economy.[5] Both when man is entirely subservient to his group and when man is entirely uprooted from his group, he loses his personal identity with the result that he cannot creatively relate himself to his fellow man, and the disintegration of human society is progressively intensified.

In order to fulfill her mission in the world today the church must "define" or "articulate," in the light of the gospel, (1) what the place of the nation is within the emerging one world community, and (2) what the place

[4] *Integrating,* not *integrated,* community.

[5] Not to *absolutize* these (or any of these) groups (e.g., Nazism, white supremacy, etc.) Christians by and large, and especially of liberal leaning, have in the past almost completely ignored the intrinsic significance of groups, and allowed those who idolize groups (i.e., totalitarian ideologists) to have their hey-day.

of the ethno-cultural community is within the increasingly pluralistic national and local societies. To proclaim the meaning of these groups in the scheme of *Heilsgeschichte* (history of salvation) is the most concrete way in which to proclaim the gospel of redemption to the world today. And this message of the church will be heard by the world only to the extent that the church herself, in various forms of her local embodiment, becomes a vital community—a community of those who have found their identities in Christ and therefore are capable of relating themselves to all people, *transcending* the racial, ethnic, cultural, and all other forms of group differences. Such a community does not ignore or gloss over group differences, but accepts people as *persons* rooted in these groups, in short, an *integrated* and integrating community. Otherwise what the church proclaims will be nothing more than "noisy gong and sounding cymbal." (I Cor. 13)

Mission to Ethnic Groups in the U.S.A. and New Nations

What we have so far considered suggests that before we go on to deliberate on what the church must do in more concrete terms we must humbly and relentlessly scrutinize what has been wrong with our missionary efforts among the American Indians, the Negro Americans, and the Oriental Americans. (See Chapter 4.) As we have already pointed out, with American Indians, we have insisted that they become like us; with American Negroes, that they stay in their place; and with Oriental Americans, that they remain aliens forever. These mistakes were made, and they are grave sins indeed in that they were our way of saying "no" to the Creator for what he has done, and as such are nothing short of *apostasy*, which was inevitable because the church had completely neglected theologically to probe the meaning of human groups, especially of ethno-cultural or racial groups.

Likewise, in dealing with the issue of the U.S. churches' mission to the emerging new nations, care must be taken lest we should be preoccupied with such concern as to find efficient techniques and methods of "helping" weak and minority churches in the otherwise pagan nations. Not to jump to any conclusion prematurely, it seems to me that the primary task for the church in the U.S.A. should be to engage in conversation with the Christian churches in all these new nations and together with them to probe what God is doing in and through their nations to his world. Here is one of the most crucial roles of the U.S. missionaries overseas, for it should most logically be through them that such an ecumenical conversation can take place among nations of widely different racial and cultural backgrounds and lead them to better understanding of each other.

Incidentally, such a corporate study will inevitably lead the Christian community to take initiative in the conversation with non-Christian communities so as to be positively involved in the common task of first asserting national identity and then of national development. Where the Christian community has been estranged from the indigenous population, it may through this process be once again rerooted in their national community. This may not, as it almost certainly will not, increase the numbers of converts or make the process of conversion any the less difficult, but Christianity will be "*indigenized*" in the true sense of the term and the Christian church prove to be a redemptive, i.e., integrating, community within that nation.

Forms of Christian Witness

What do all these considerations add up to?

First of all, it is clear beyond the shadow of a doubt that the church's witness in the area of race relations is not to run an "ambulance service," or to be engaged in "charity work" for the victims of racial injustices, or to attack the social structure which has built-in discriminations, by way of legislative activity and many other organized or unorganized group actions. All these are terribly important and Christians as citizens are under obligation to take as active a part as humanly possible in one or all of these activities, which inevitably means personal involvement in many a civic, social, and political action of secular or supra-religious orientation. The church as the church has a unique mission of her own in reference to race relations as well as to all other human problems, social or personal, over and above proclaiming the will of God and exhorting people to obey it. What that mission is has been discussed in the preceding pages. Now how can or should it be carried out?

Whatever else it may be, the church's mission should not deliberately try to *wipe out* racial differences and ethnic distinctions. The vital principle underlying the concept of integration is not the mixing up of races so as to assimilate them into something like one neutralized super-race. Why not? Because such is totally unnecessary, for mankind is already one and always has been. In the true sense of the term there is only one race, the human race, and therefore there is no need trying to obliterate all the lesser groupings that do exist within one family of the human race.

This means that a racially integrated society can only be one in which ethno-racial differences have ceased to be a determining factor in the area of human relationships. It is a society in which, when one hires a worker; buys or sells a house; chooses a neighborhood to live in, or a university to attend; rides on a bus or airplane; contracts marriage; goes to see a show or goes on a picnic in groups —wherever and whenever one has to relate himself to other people in one capacity or another, their racial or ethnic background does not play any decisive role in one's decision-making process. One loves, respects, associates, and does business with this or that person, neither *in spite of* nor *because of* what they ethno-racially are, but simply because they are fellow humans.

This situation is possible only in a society in which everybody accepts himself as he is and for what he is and accepts others as they are and for what they are. The opposite is a society which compels members of one ethnic group categorically to exclude, from the sphere of his inter-personal and social relationships, all the members of another ethnic group—such a society makes it humanly impossible for anybody to accept himself and everybody else as and for what he is. This, as we have seen earlier in Chapters 6 and 7, is precisely what is wrong with our society today. Unless it becomes racially integrated—and integrating—most citizens will eventually be inwardly fragmented and disintegrated.

Would I suggest, then, that the church should do nothing about the race problem? Do I not sound as if I think that the major trouble with us is that we take the matter of race too seriously? I really do. Most of us indeed take it far too seriously, much more seriously than it deserves. In fact many of us are so preoccupied with our neighbors' race that we fail to see his person—we see him and are near him and yet we do not *meet* him at all! Only as we are able to be a little more relaxed about it, learn to take it more casually and with a bit more humor, will most of the racial problems begin to disappear.

I am also fully aware that our society simply does not permit us to be relaxed about, or to take more casually with light-hearted humor, the matter of race relations. We just have to accept the tragic reality of our society and accordingly I do not for one moment suggest that all the church has to do is to admonish people to do nothing about the matter, and instead sit back and relax.

What we do and how we do it must be determined by what we aim at. Means are indeed shaped by ends. The basic trouble with the church in the area of race relations has been that those who are in the position of leadership and responsibility have seldom known in precise practical terms what the church should be striving to achieve. Not knowing *where* to go, how can one decide *how* to go? Where to go, not in the millennium but within one's life time, must be determined in the light of where we are, how and why we got here, and the direction toward which ultimately we should reach.

What is uniquely the church's task is a threefold thing—that is, one task with three dimensions: (1) that her professional ministry stay in conversation with all segments of the society or every group within its populace; (2) that her membership as a corporate body constitute a community in which people representing all sorts of groups in society at large stay in conversation with one another; and (3) that all the churches in the given society combine their forces to provide an institutional framework within which all segments of citizenry can be constantly engaged in open conversation with one another.

The central key to all these is to keep *conversation* going, within the framework of prayer and worship, among all the existing groups so that they stay in communication one with another, be they racial or ethnic groups, opinion-groups, vested interest groups, political groups, or what ever else. Where inter-group communication has been completely broken down, the first task for the church is that of restoring it, for without it all the other things done in the interest of good race relations will be little more than a stop-gap operation. To perform this task the church herself must be a racially integrated community (in the sense expounded in the preceding pages), and where such is not the case the church had better take care of the situation, however painful a price she may have to pay for it, *for only an integrated community can be an integrating community in the midst of a disintegrated society of men.*

EPILOGUE

Race Relations in Biblical Perspective

In this epilogue I wish to spell out the church's message to modern man who is caught in group tensions and antagonisms.

Bible, the Book of the Church

The church's message in its totality is contained in the Bible, not in a few select passages but in the Bible as a whole. The Bible is *the* book of the church in the sense that it is the foundation upon which the church stands and also the official testimony by which the church bears witness to her Lord and Master.

The Bible as a whole tells us as much about the condition of human existence as about God. In the Bible human history is the context in which God-in-action is seen, in whose light the truth about man is revealed. Human history in the Bible is presented in terms of the history of Israel, a peculiar *people* chosen by God to represent the whole of mankind.

The history of Israel unfolds itself around two foci—the exodus event in the Old Testament and the death and resurrection of Jesus in the New. Exodus and the death-resurrection of Jesus must not be read in isolation. Together, the history of God's deliverance of Israel from bondage and the history of God Incarnate reveal the singleness of God's redemptive purpose for his church, seen first as the Israel of the Old Testament and then in the Christian Church of the New.

The Church in the Bible

The church, according to the Bible, is a people called into being by God, "a chosen race, a royal priesthood, a holy nation, God's own people, who . . . once were no people but now are God's people." (1 Pet. 2:9-10, cf., story of Abraham, Gen. Chs. 12 ff.) God chose them as a people for the purpose of bringing back to himself the world which he created according to his own design (creation story, Gen. 1-2), which, however, in the course of time has been estranged from him (story of the lost Paradise, Gen. 3) and torn to pieces (story of Cain and Abel, Gen. 4); story of the flood and descendants of Noah (Gen. 6-10); story of the Tower of Babel (Gen. 11). To restore the once-lost unity of mankind and present it back to God is the task God has set for his church (2 Cor. 5:18-20; Eph. 2:11-22; Rom. 5:10; Col. 1:20; etc.) This task is described severally by the church as "reconciliation," "redemption," "atonement," etc.

The history of the old Israel, from Abraham to the restoration of Jerusalem after the Babylonian exile, is the story of Israel's engagement in the task of reconciliation. As a people specially chosen by God, Israel was set apart—a stranger among peoples of the world (Heb. 11:13; 1 Pet.

2:11). Through their bitter experiences as strangers, despised, rejected and oppressed, they learned their God-given mission to restore the once-lost unity of mankind, which was to be achieved by relating themselves in love and forgiveness to the very peoples among whom they sojourn as foreigners. "You shall not oppress a stranger; you know the heart of a stranger, for you were strangers in the land of Egypt." (Exod. 23:9; also 22:21) Or, again, "When a stranger sojourns with you in your land, you shall not do him wrong. The stranger who sojourns with you shall be to you as the native among you, and you shall love him as yourself; for you were strangers in the land of Egypt; I am the Lord your God." (Lev. 19:33-34; also Deut. 10:19)

The Shema

It was in the context of their experience as an alien people that the old Israel received the injunction: "You shall love your neighbor as yourself" (Lev. 19:18), which the new Israel equated with another injunction, the Shema: "Hear, O Israel: The Lord our God is one Lord, and you shall love the Lord your God with all your heart, and with all your soul, and with all your might." (Deut. 6:4-5, cf. Matt. 22:37; Mark 12:29-30; Luke 10:27) The point is that as God's chosen people, they were to love, not only those who belonged to them and to whom they belonged, but also those who were strangers to them and to whom they were strangers. This they learned through their bitter experience of Egyptian bondage and their consequent deliverance—not by their own power, might or device, but by God's grace.

Unity of Mankind in the Old Testament

Thus the old Israel's belief in the basic oneness of mankind was based upon their encounter with all sorts of people as strangers. Israel, like all other nations in antiquity, was a tightly knit, closed community bound by blood relations. As the story of Abraham seeking a wife for his son Isaac from among his kinsmen afar indicates, and as has since been reiterated notably by Ezra and Nehemiah in the most extreme fashion, Israel has been zealous to maintain its ethnic or national identity, for its survival as a people was constantly at stake. All other nations were either enemies or potential enemies of Israel.

Ethnic tensions and inter-group strifes were the normal state of affairs with them all, and yet Israel was led again and again to see the oneness of all mankind. "God created man in his own image . . . male and female he created them." (Gen. 1:27) Many a geneology, from those of Adam (Gen. 5), Noah (Gen. 10) and his three sons (Gen. 11), to that of Jesus (Matt. 1 and Luke 3), testifies to the persistent faith of Israel in the basic oneness of all mankind. When nationalistic spirit mounted in the face of serious national crisis, they countered these trends with such stories as the Book of Ruth or the Book of Jonah reiterating the oneness of all peoples. It is against this background that we can begin to appreciate the real import of what Jesus said:

"You have heard that it was said, 'You shall love your neighbor and hate your enemy.' But I say to you, Love your enemies and pray for those who persecute you, so that you may be sons of your Father who is in heaven." (Matt. 5:43-45)

Thus, for all its emphasis upon the ethnic identity of Israel, the Bible is anything but racist literature.

Enemy

For Jesus as in the tradition of Israel, "enemy" is but a passing phase of one's relationship to a person or a people. Enmity between two parties is in fact an indication that the twain have to exist in relation to each other, otherwise conflict would not have occurred between them. When, therefore, a stranger appears before you, it is better to face him as a potential friend or neighbor. According to an old Japanese proverb, "Your brother is the first stranger you will meet in your life." Cain and Abel, representing the early nomadic hunting and agrarian cultures, committed the first recorded murder—between two brothers! From this early account of fratricide the Hebrew tradition came somehow to see a brother even in an enemy.

Who Is My Neighbor?

So it was that Jesus told the remarkable story of the good Samaritan to that sophisticated intellectual who, "desiring to justify himself," asked, "And who is my neighbor?" Jesus concluded his story by asking, "Which of these three, do you think, proved neighbor to the man . . . ?" (Luke 10:25-37) Neighbor, like enemy, is not a fixed status. One can be either a neighbor or an enemy to any and every person, far and near, known and unknown, of same or different race, nationality, color, or religion, seen or unseen, especially in the microcosmic world in which we are living today. But one cannot remain forever unrelated, always a stranger.

One cannot stay within one's own circle, the closed community of one's own kind, and look for one's potential neighbors only among the "insiders" of one's group. Rather, Jesus commands us to *go* out and become a neighbor to every man, regardless of the group to which he belongs. This is the command of Jesus and his church to those who profess to be Christians and members of his Body: "Go and do likewise."

Strangers and Exiles

We are destined to be "strangers and exiles on the earth" (Heb. 11:13) for the sake of the task God has committed to us, namely to reintegrate the world which is now broken by racial and ethnic tensions and inter-group conflicts. We are not to stay within the circle of our friends, not even the circle of Christian fellowships, but, like Abraham, we are under our Master's order to "go from your country and your kindred and your father's house to the land that I will show you." (Gen. 12:1)

Like Christ, his Body the church is a stranger and exile upon the earth, identifying itself with all races and peoples who are estranged from God. It is by virtue of this identity that the church is enabled to be an integrating community —a third race.

Primacy of Relationship

Relationship, therefore, is of ultimate importance. Where broken relationships between groups, or between persons, are allowed to remain unrepaired, everyone suffers. (Matt. 5:23-26) Jesus emphasized this in many parables. Take, for example, that of the so-called prodigal son. (Luke 15) Dr.

John Karefa-Smart of Sierra Leone once said that to call this parable by that name betrays the basic bias of Western Christians. Africans would have called it "parable of a broken family." Some called this the "parable of the waiting father," which is an improvement over "parable of the prodigal son." But in my opinion, my African friend has come closest to the heart of Jesus' message.

"Not many days later, the younger son . . . took his journey to a far country, and there he squandered his property in loose living." Thus the relationships that bound this young man to his father and brother were broken, not necessarily for unsavory reasons; perhaps he wished only to prove his independence or his ability to govern his own life. With the breach of relationships, even in the name of freedom and independence, however, the youth has become a man without identity!

What was his sin? Not his squandering his property in loose living, which is a result of his sin. What drove him to that is sin, namely breaking himself loose from the relationships in which he has the root of his personality—estrangement from the ground of his very being.

This, of course, is precisely what some members of minority groups are apt to do. Being somehow made to feel ashamed of the group with which they are identified—and with wishful thinking that somewhere in a far country, completely dissociated from their own group, they might possibly find happiness in freedom and independence—they try to reject their own groups. With such a breach of relationship with their own group, they lose their identity. And the society which has permitted them to take such a step has also to suffer, like the father of the prodigal.

Restoration of Broken Relationships

Where relationships have been permitted to remain broken for a long time, their restoration is both difficult and costly. But who pays the price? According to Jesus it is the church. Even as he paid with his own life, the church must pay the required price with its life. The parable of the "king who wished to settle accounts with his servants" (Matt. 18:23-25) shows how important it is to maintain unbroken the relationships which have been established, whether between persons or between groups. "Out of pity for him the Lord of that servant released him and forgave him the debt." Here the party who has been wronged is paying the price in behalf of the party who has done the wrong, for the relationships that existed between the king and his servant were infinitely more important or precious to him than all the money his servant owed him. Therefore, when this same servant dared to sacrifice his relationships with one of his co-workers over a small debt, the king "in anger delivered him to the jailors, till he should pay his debts."

Forgiveness: Relationship-Restoring Power

Forgiveness is a dynamic force that restores broken relationships. The emphasis on forgiveness in the teaching of Jesus stems from the fact that every man is inexplicably related to every other man. Nevertheless, many otherwise religious persons find it difficult or repulsive to accept certain people and be accepted by them simply because they belong to different groups from one's own.

It is not, however, mainly those who are total strangers to

us that we find most difficult to accept and love. Hostility and enmity are usually directed more toward those to whom we are already related, or in whose life we are sufficiently involved to find some cause for our irritation and apprehension. Hence, "love your enemy," says Jesus—learn to love the man you know well enough to hate!

The Case of Group Antagonism

There is a subtle point in the parable of the good Samaritan. The hero of the story forgave the man in distress his being a Jew, and in so doing he was asking that his being a Samaritan be forgiven by the Jewish man too, so that they could enter into genuine human relationships unhampered by their nationalities. To notice that the man lying on the roadside wounded was a Jew makes him no longer a stranger to the Samaritan—they are enemies to each other, not because they personally have a grudge against each other but because of history! To discover that they are enemies to each other is to acknowledge that they cannot go on having nothing to do with each other, for relationships, though impaired, are there to bind them together.

The ethnic group which gives each man his identity as a human person is the very thing which keeps men apart. But remaining apart from each other they will be less than what God intends them to be. Man needs to be proud of the group which gives him his identity. But the moment this pride gets in the way of his relating himself to people of other groups, he must ask to be forgiven his being what he is! This does not mean that we should forget what we are, for none of us can be what we are apart from our ethnic or national heritage. Only it must not be made the object of idolatry. "Go therefore and make disciples of all nations. . . ." (Matt. 28-19) The church is sent into the world to make the *nations* to be what they are supposed to be, so that each of them may fulfill its vocation—to give an identity to its citizens. The church's mission to a nation is inseparable from that to the individual persons therein involved, for each person must be dealt with as a whole person rooted in his nation.

Love in the New Testament

To relate oneself to others—this is what the New Testament means by the term "to love." "We know that we have passed out of death into life, because we love the brethren. . . . He who does not love remains in death. Any one who hates his brother is a murderer." (1 John 3:14-15) To love is to live in fellowship, while to hate is to die and to kill. Love is a power that enables man to relate himself to his fellow men; it is *the* community-creating and relationship-sustaining force. It is of utmost importance to note that Paul's famous passage (1 Cor. 13) comes in the middle of his discussion on the Holy Spirit and the Christian Community. (1 Cor. 12-14)

The Holy Spirit enables men of all nations "who were heathen and led astray to dumb idols" to say, "Jesus is Lord"—that is, to accept Jesus as the supreme Lord and sovereign king who reigns over all nations. (12:2-3) The same Spirit gives different men different gifts—what one might call "specialized skills"—which distinguish some men and, in practice, tend to separate them from others. This separation, however, ought not to happen in the church, for with Christ as the sovereign king all men are united into one. "For by one Spirit we were all baptized into one body—Jews or Greeks, slaves or free—and all were made to drink of one Spirit." (12:13)

What is it that keeps united this newly constituted corporate body of men—the Body of Christ, the church? Surely it is not the specialized functions of its various officers or the specialized tasks of professionally trained workers among its members. It can only be *love,* the "most excellent" of all the gifts of the Holy Spirit. Without love, the binding force that relates one man to another and keeps the human community intact, all is nothing. Love is not a virtue but a force—a power that enables one to stay related, to seek relationships with the strange or hostile and the unlovable. Love enables the mortal eyes to have a glimpse, however dimly and fragmentarily, of the ultimate truth of manhood under God.

Faith

Love thus understood is the self-manifestation of faith, or faith-in-action. Faith "is the assurance of things hoped for, the conviction of things not seen," by which "the men of old received divine approval." (Heb. 11:1) Faith is what enables us to know that "God in Christ has reconciled the world to himself" (2 Cor. 5:18), and "has put all things under his feet and has made him the head over all things for the church, which is his body." (Eph. 1:22 ff.) Faith is what enables us, with the author of Ephesians, bold to say: "He [God] destined us in love to be his sons through Christ. . . . For he has made known to us . . . the mystery of his will . . . as a plan for the fullness of time, to unite all things in him, things in heaven and things on earth." (Eph. 1:5-10)

To be Christian is to become incorporated in the Body of Christ. (Eph. 2:15) We who were once "alienated from the commonwealth of Israel, and strangers to the covenants of promise" have now been made "fellow citizens with the saints and members of the household of God, built upon the foundations of the apostles and prophets, Christ Jesus himself being the chief cornerstone, in whom the whole structure is joined together. . . ." (Eph. 2:11-22) This means that we Christians are the church in the world, God's agents of his ministry of reconciliation, whose mission is to restore in love the unity of God's world and bring it back to him as a reintegrated whole.

The Church: the Body of Christ

As members of the church we have been given a new identity. "For as many of you as were baptized into Christ have put on Christ. There is neither Jew nor Greek, there is neither male nor female; for you are all one in Christ Jesus. And if you are Christ's, then you are Abraham's offspring. . . ." (Gal. 3:27-29) "If anyone is in Christ, he is a new creation. . . . So we are ambassadors of Christ, God making his appeal through us." (2 Cor. 5:17-20)

We therefore no longer regard men from a human point of view and say, "He is a Negro, he is a Jew, he is an Oriental." From a human point of view Christ was a Jew—a Palestinian Jew of the first century—but in faith, he is the risen Lord, the sovereign king over all mankind (cf., 2 Cor. 5:16). "No one can say 'Jesus is Lord' except by the Holy Spirit." (1 Cor. 12:3) Christians are those, according to the imagery of the Revelation of John, who were "sealed out of every tribe of the sons of Israel," no longer to be identified by their tribes but by "the Seal of God upon their forehead." (Rev. 7:3 ff.; 9:4)

To put it differently, a man without Christ is a citizen of one nation only. A man incorporated into the Body of Christ belongs to two nations. He belongs to the whole of mankind as well as to the nation or the family into which he happens to have been born. This is what baptism really means.

Baptism

Within the community of baptism, the only thing that matters is the Christian name, given in baptism "wherein I was made a member of Christ, the child of God, and an inheritor of the kingdom of heaven." That is, my life is now so oriented that my race, my nationality, my kinship group, and all other groups to which I belong, are transcended. With this name I belong to the church universal and through it to the whole human race.

In this light to be a Christian means that we *Christianly* relate ourselves to every person in the world, whether he be a Christian or not, for we have realized that all mankind is one household of God, in which everybody is related to everybody else, though divided on the surface and for the time being. Christians are not to ignore anyone's race, nationality, etc., but are to face each person *as he is in his totality*—that is, as a person rooted in his group(s) with a give name all his own. The only question which is pertinent for a Christian to ask as he faces another person is, "What is your name?" Neither religion, nor race, nor nationality should make any difference in a Christian's attitude toward another human being.

Who Belongs to Mankind?

The destruction of *all* in-groups is an indispensable step toward the ultimate unity of mankind. The church as a redemptive community can never be a cozy in-group of "the saved," but must always be an *integrating* and open community in which persons from diverse and sundry groups are united in mutual respect and love.

"Am I my brother's keeper?" "Who is my neighbor?" In these two questions are represented two negative forces operating in every in-group—the self-destroying force from within and the will to keep outsiders out. Rigidly established, tightly knit closed groups are thus cancers destroying the growth and development of a wholesome human community in which everybody is accepted as a brother and a neighbor by everyone else.

In Christ there really are no strangers, no outsiders, no minorities, for all are *neighbors* even in their anonymity. This is the holy anonymity of God himself, who is no "respecter of persons" but loves all men equally and absolutely and wills that all live in peace with one another on earth, which may once again be fair in his sight.

A NOTE ABOUT THE FORMAT

The text of this book is set in Linotype Caledonia, 10 point leaded 3 points. Designed by the late W. A. Dwiggins, this face belongs to the "modern" family of type faces and is somewhat similar to Scotch Modern, although more freely drawn than that letter.

Manufactured by Sowers Printing Company,
Lebanon, Pa.
Paper covers by Affiliated Lithographers, Inc.,
New York
Paper: S. D. Warren's #66 Antique
Typographic design by Margery W. Smith

600 F.W.